INFLUENCE AND PERSUASION

THE PSYCHOLOGY OF LEADERSHIP AND HUMAN BEHAVIOR

JONATHAN GREEN

DRAGON GOD BOOKS

Copyright © 2017 by Dragon God, Inc.

All rights reserved.

Simultaneously published in United States of America, the UK, India, Germany, France, Italy, Canada, Japan, Spain, and Brazil.

All rights reserved. No part of this book may be reproduced in any form or by any other electronic or mechanical means – except in the case of brief quotations embedded in articles or reviews –without written permission from its author.

Influence and Persuasion has provided the most accurate information possible. Many of the techniques used in this book are from personal experiences. The author shall not be held liable for any damages resulting from use of this book.

Paperback ISBN-13: 978-1548781316

Paperback ISBN-10: 1548781312

Hardback ISBN: 978-1947667082

To Those Who Strive to Lead

CONTENTS

What is your Current Influence Level?	vii
Introduction	ix
Who Am I?	xi
Just a Regular Guy	xiii
About This Book	xv
Additional Content	xvii
1. What is Leadership?	1
2. Creating Shared Values and Vision	17
3. The Art of Persuasion	21
4. Creation of a Positive Workplace Culture	39
5. Team Dynamics	46
6. Communication	52
7. Fostering Loyalty	66
8. Your Personal Development as a Leader	75
What We've Learned	87
The End is Just Another Beginning	91
Did you Take the Assessment?	93
More Information	94
Found a Typo?	95
About the Author	97
Books by Jonathan Green	99
Adult Coloring Books by Jonathan Green and ArtOfColoringBook.com	101
One Last Thing	103

WHAT IS YOUR CURRENT INFLUENCE LEVEL?

https://servenomaster.com/persuasive

Thank you for purchasing *Influence and Persuasion*.

Before we start to improve the power of your influence, we need to know where you are starting.

This little two-minute quiz will give you your score on the Influence Index, and by the end of this book, we will raise that score!

What is your Current Influence Level?

Please take this assessment before and after reading the book.

https://servenomaster.com/persuasive

INTRODUCTION

Influence is one of those words that often remain elusive and ill-defined. If you tried to visualize the meaning of influence in your mind, you might see:

- A Fortune 500 CEO
- A hypnotist
- A dictator
- A teacher

Some of these visualizations have positive connotations, and some are quite negative. When I close my eyes, I see an evil hypnotist trying to put me under his spell; possibly trying to learn my PIN code!

I hope that you didn't grab this book expecting to learn how to coax PIN codes from the subconsciousness minds of strangers; you will be sorely disappointed and may just want to return this book right now!

In this book, we will focus on the best type of influence. It's not just about getting your way or getting people to give you things – influence is so much more than that. With real influence, people will beg you to take their money, and they will seek out your wisdom and advice constantly. You will become a magnet for success, and you will have no choice but to raise the price of your time. It's the only way you can handle wielding so much power.

Anybody can force someone to do something against their will; all you need is the threat of violence. But the second you turn around, they will turn on you. Ruling through fear never lasts and it's far harder.

There is an easier path.

WHO AM I?

I live and die based on the power of my influence. I live on a tiny island in the South Pacific, and my ability to set up deals and partnerships determines if my children get to eat this month.

I'm most well known as the creator of the Networking Empire course, which covers the entire process of forming an army of fans, supporters, and business partners. My ability to find people to work with caused my income to increase twenty-fold in just twelve months.

Living on a tropical island does not mean that I live in isolation by any means. Today, I'm in Los Angeles for a massive conference. It's my first time in the West in over two years. I bought a temporary SIM card yesterday, and people are already texting me like crazy to make sure they get a few minutes of face time with me. Models, millionaires, and titans of industry all seek my wisdom.

JUST A REGULAR GUY

If you have the paperback version of this book, you can flip to the back cover of this book to see what I look like. In the digital versions, you have to skip forward to the "About the Author" section. Take a quick look. I'm nothing special to look at. I don't have a Silicon Valley tan, and my parents didn't give me my start in business. I'm just a regular guy who created influence from nothing to build his own tropical empire.

Looks, money, and power come after influence, not before. No matter where you are in life, we can increase your influence to get you better results in any area, from love to finance. I have advised celebrity chefs, hedge fund managers, actors, and leadership trainers. I have dated famous musicians, international models, and professional athletes. I will share my secret in this short book. (Hint: it's definitely **not** my looks.)

Most books on influence and executive leadership start by talking about the importance of height. If that really makes a difference, then I'm in big trouble. I'm 5'9, and even though I exercise every day, I most often get compared to fat comedians...and occasionally fat race car drivers or golfers. Every few years, it's a new comedian, but it's never anyone skinny. None of that superficial stuff matters. All that matters is your ability to grow, cultivate, and wield influence.

ABOUT THIS BOOK

Before we can start this book, we need to lock in a destination. Now that we know your current Influence Index, we have our starting point. That's great, but that doesn't get you excited. I don't get excited my first day at the gym; I want to know how I'm going to look in ninety days!

By the end of this book, you will have a deep understanding of what influence really means. Instead of a cartoon image in the back of your brain, you will have a clearly defined set of characteristics and attributes that you can use to assess the Influence Index of those around you. When you were in high school, you never thought about influence – what you wanted was popularity.

Popularity is another measure of influence. Popularity is the ability to get other people to like you. Sounds a little Machiavellian, doesn't it? The ability to become popular and form a real connection with new friends is now within your grasp. In this book, we are going to unlock the power of popularity. If you have children that are still in school, feel free to share these lessons with them. You will become their new hero.

This is not a book of theory, philosophy, or opinion. I don't care how things work in the lab; I only care how they work in the real world. As a researcher, I'm a street fighter. I like to get in the mud and see what happens. If I can't use a technique myself to make something unbelievable happen, then that technique is garbage to me. I'm not here to teach you the believable, that's far too boring. I'm here to teach you the unbelievable.

As I sit in a hotel room I didn't pay for, fresh off a flight I didn't pay for, and about to spend a weekend closing seven-figure deals at a conference I didn't pay to attend, I can only say that your life is about to change for the better. Stick with me for this short guide, and I will bend reality for you.

ADDITIONAL CONTENT

Throughout this book I mention other books, images, links, and additional content. All of that can be found at:

https://servenomaster.com/influencer

You don't have to worry about trying to remember any other links or the names of anything mentioned in this book. Just enjoy the journey and focus on taking control of your destiny.

1
WHAT IS LEADERSHIP?

I went to college at the University of Richmond. One of the big selling points of that campus tour I took seventeen years ago was their school of leadership. Yes. At my college, you could actually major in leadership. Looking back, I can only thank my stars that I didn't waste my time on such a silly major.

Would you let a twenty-two-year-old kid walk into your company and become the boss on day one because he majored in leadership? I hope not. Sitting in a bunch of classes is the worst way to learn leadership. All the kids in that major were nothing compared to the guys in ROTC. The military is one of the best places to learn about leadership. It's the real crucible.

Every day, we hear about the importance of effective leadership, but nobody really knows how to do it. If you know how to wield influence, then leadership is the natural successor. Books that focus on leadership often skip that core principle, and if you've ever tried to master leadership in the past and been left floundering, that's why.

Every day, we have hundreds of opportunities to expand our influence and demonstrate our ability to lead. It's the small things that define us. If I can't trust you not to steal a lunch from the refrigerator in the break room, how on earth can I trust you with a company car or a corner office?

The little decisions we make that don't count, or the things we do when nobody's looking, are the most important moments in your life. Your personality is made up of thousands of small decisions. A hero isn't someone who goes out looking to do something amazing; it's someone who, in a moment of great import, makes the right decision. It's the culmination of thousands of little decisions in a moment of crisis.

The Day I Was Nearly Sentenced to Death

You don't really know who you are until you are under pressure. Many years ago, I was dating a woman in a foreign country. One day, the police kicked in the door to arrest us for violating the religion of the country. We weren't married, and it was a sin for us to be alone in my hotel room. The punishment in that country was twenty-five years in prison. For a foreigner, that is a death sentence. If they had put me into that prison, I would have died there. Even if I managed to hang on, I would still be there today.

The head detective looked at me and said, "This woman looks like a prostitute. She says she is your girlfriend, but if she's a prostitute we can put her in jail tonight and behead her in the morning, and you'll be free to go. You're just a foreigner that was tricked by a wily woman. Just say the word, and you're free to go."

You don't know who you are until your integrity is put to the test. Would you give your life for someone that you'd known for less than a week? It's easy to say yes, but is it the truth? In that moment, I was in my own crucible. A day earlier, I could not have predicted what I would do next.

I was sitting there, thinking about how close each border of this country was. This little country borders the only three countries on earth that are even worse: all three of them were in active civil wars at the time. There was no escape, and certainly no calling my embassy for help. They would have sent someone to take a polaroid of me before my execution and waved goodbye.

What do you do when the price of integrity is your life? Is that a tax you are willing to pay or will you break?

Looking back, I still can't believe what happened. I stuck to my guns, and I defended her innocence. Staring death in the eye, I did not blink. I said she was my girlfriend and that we were innocent. They split us up and made us sweat. Two hours later, when it was looking like the sun was about to set on the life of Jonathan Green, they let us go.

The head detective looked me in the eye and said, "You are a man of honor. You may go."

No bribe. No calls to the embassy. A solution that I did not know existed presented itself. I was rewarded for my integrity. I survived the Kobayashi Maru.

I do not recommend that you take this same test. A million factors came together that day to save my life. If it happened again, I doubt I would walk out of it alive. And in case you're wondering, that woman is not my wife. I only dated her a few more weeks and realized that she was awful. It was not a test of our relationship; it was a test of my integrity. That is very different.

When people question my integrity or sense of self, I can only laugh. I had that moment in my life where I was tested, and I discovered a will of iron that I didn't know existed until that day.

In every life, we have moments where we can choose greatness or cowardice. If your past is littered with poor decisions, it's not too late. We can turn it around. It's never too late to unlock the greatness within you.

Brainstorming Exercise

This isn't a silly college course. This book is about becoming a leader. With that in mind, I'd like you to take a moment and think about what it means to be a leader. As with all the books in this series, I recommend that you use a journal to write down your thoughts and notes. I have a spiral notebook next to me all the time.

1. What are the characteristics of an effective leader?
2. What qualities should a leader have and which ones should a leader never have?

Take the time to think about this before jumping ahead to read my answer. This isn't about guessing; it's about finding out who you are. The more you participate in the activities, the better your results will be.

Once you feel comfortable with your list, you can move on to the next section.

Characteristics of an Effective Leader

This list is not organized by priority or power. It is not alphabetical. It's impossible to weight or prioritize the qualities of leadership, so please don't look for a deeper meaning in the order of this section. Instead, look within yourself and find the qualities that you have mastered and those that still need a little work.

1. Delegation

Delegation is an interesting place to start. Most despots dream of delegation. To them, it is the ability to order other people around, but they are wrong. This skill is about knowing the strengths of a team. You know how to divide up a task and who to assign for each component?

Most definitions of delegation are so trite. They explain what it means but not how to do it. How can you find out what people are good at and where they excel? This key step is the beginning of everything.

The core aphorism of my business is:

Find out what people want and give it to them.

This applies to every single area of life. Before it's time for you to delegate a project, get to know the members of the team. Ask them what they like to work on. I will simply ask, "What are you good at and what do you like to do?"

This one question will provide you with all the data you need to delegate, even to a room full of strangers.

2. Communication

Telling people what to do is pretty awesome, but you can't do that until you learn how to listen. When you think of communication as a leader, start with your ear before you think of your mouth.

I met President Bill Clinton when I was in high school. I was in downtown Nashville, and about a thousand police officers suddenly appeared. Two minutes later, he was walking up and down the line shaking hands. Of course, I stuck my hand out. Who doesn't want to shake hands with a president?

People often say that he had the ability to make you feel like the most important person in the room. That was the secret to his success. He made everyone feel important. That comes from listening; the more you listen, the more influence you will accrue.

3. Commitment

Anyone can set a goal, but can you stick to it? Will you stay the course or will you follow the next butterfly that distracts you? If you can't see a project through to the finish line, nobody will want to join you for that journey. Your ability to finish projects demonstrates that you are a leader worth following. Finishing on time is also a big part of this.

4. Creativity

I love reading science fiction novels. In epic space battles, it is the captain who comes up with the unexpected battle plan that saves the day. The ability to invent a brand-new tactic or way to use technology saves humanity from the alien hordes.

You don't have to be this creative to lead. My creativity is much less glamourous, but I can talk to anyone and, within five minutes, find a way to triple their income. I can assess their skills, talents, and passions, and offer them a path to success. This comes from my imagination as much as it comes from experience. Looking at a problem from a unique angle and seeing opportunity where other people see obstacle is one of the signs of a great leader.

5. Integrity

In a restaurant, they use the same ketchup bottles for years. Whenever the ketchup runs low in a bottle, they crack open the industrial ketchup barrel and refill. But there is another way to refill. You can just add water to the bottle.

I bet you did this to your dad's whiskey when you were in high school. A little water in the mix and nobody will know the difference.

Integrity is what you do when nobody is looking. In these days of intense politics, I always look at the person before I look at their policy. If someone talks about hating walls and borders, I check to see if they have one around their house. Do they live in a gated community? The reason we all hate politicians is simple.

They say one thing and do another.

They have the unique ability to live without integrity and still look at themselves in the mirror every morning. Nobody thinks that politicians are honest. That's insanity. They have a complete and total lack of integrity – it's one of the great tragedies of our society, but it's reality.

You can be better. If you are someone who does the same thing, even when nobody is looking, you will be a great leader. Is your public persona your true self or simply an affectation?

6. Confidence

Would you buy a car from someone who thought it was garbage? Then why would you follow a leader who doesn't believe in themselves?

Every once in a while, I get a book review that hates on me for being in love with myself. These bad reviewers hate that I use myself in my examples and think that my biography shouldn't use the word "I" even once. That's a pretty critical review!

I could justify or explain my writing style, but I don't need to. People are always going to love you or hate you. Just do your best, and the rest will sort itself out. That's true confidence.

When you combine experience with effort, you unlock limitless confidence. I know that this book will be a bestseller. All my books are. I have done this over fifty times. My experience gives me the confidence to make a bold statement that some people would find pretentious. People of low confidence can't tell the difference, but you can, and that's why people are going to follow you.

I'm not very good-looking or very tall. The secret to my dating success is pure confidence. I can stand in a crowded bar or club and, if I'm not talking, I do not exist. You could ask every single person in there about me, and none of them will have seen me. I'm a social ghost. It's not a weakness; it's one of my greatest superpowers. I can get close and observe social connections point blank. Don't get caught up thinking I'm complaining about my looks – focus on the message here.

All of my confidence is internal. It comes from within, not from strangers. The moment I start talking, my confidence becomes the force of gravity, and it pulls people towards me. That belief in myself is the key to everything.

Sometimes, standing in a bar, I will see men who are very loud (if you're a woman, please forgive me, but I rarely compare myself to women). They are taller, better-looking, and richer than me. They wear expensive clothes and talk loudly about all their accomplishments in life. They need to show everyone how confident they are.

When I start talking to a beautiful woman, one of these men always walks up. He's a friend or a coworker, and this is where something very interesting happens. Most men look at me like I'm nothing. They spend a few minutes and decide I'm not worth the effort of competing with, and they walk away. I'm not loud, therefore I must not be confident.

A few guys notice that I have something going on below the surface, and they go on the attack. They get louder or intentionally mess up my name and try to demonstrate how strong they are.

This brashness is a level of confidence. Unfortunately for them, this is only the second level of confidence. There is a higher level they don't know about, and it's all about quiet confidence.

The stories about me in this book are ones that I never tell in person. This is an educational book, and I prefer to use real examples from my life when I teach principles. But if you were having a drink with me in person, I would spend the entire time asking about you.

You don't need to be loud. You just need to believe in yourself. Confidence doesn't come from how other people perceive you; it comes from within.

7. Positive

The very first time I launched a product with a partner online, he killed the business with one email. It was a few hours into the release of our product, and he emailed every single person we knew a letter that started with the following sentence: "Our launch has one foot in the grave, what can we do to save it?"

Here's the surprise ending. Every single one of them cut ties with the launch and stopped sending us customers. You don't put up a "going out of business" sign directly below your "grand opening" sign.

This guy ended up stealing a great deal of money from me, so I don't mind using him as a negative example. His negativity killed that business. When you only see the dark cloud, nobody wants to be around you.

8. Inspirational

I would love to pretend that I know everything about leadership, but that would be so disingenuous. There is always somebody smarter. Teaching you how to be inspirational is just tough.

We all want to be inspirational, but it's hard to "become inspirational" from one day to the other.

If you stick to the core principle of integrity, over time you will become inspirational to other people. This is the culmination of all the other good things that you do. While you can't practice being an inspirational leader, you can develop the habits that will turn you into one.

9. Intuitive

Intuition is another word that sounds good but is hard to explain. It's like telling you to be lucky. I don't believe in luck; I believe in manipulating the odds. The best way to improve your intuition is through experience and study. Spend time with mentors and other successful people and ask them how they make decisions.

They make decisions based on a logic that to an outsider may look like magic or intuition.

10. Educated

We can debate book smarts vs. street smarts all day. Education isn't about how many letters you have after your name; it's about how you approach knowledge. Are you still seeking new knowledge or have you learned everything there is to know?

I would never go to a doctor who stopped learning twenty years ago. I have a thirst for knowledge that I know you have as well – it drove you to buy this book. The desire to keep learning is a core sign of a natural leader. I'm always looking to absorb new information and then share it as quickly as possible.

Most people in our society stop learning when they graduate from high school. Like a badge of honor, they will tell anyone who will listen that they haven't read a book in seventeen years. That badge of honor is keeping them from becoming a leader.

When you read all the time, you can easily impress one of these people. You just remember a few little facts from a book you read last month, but to them, you seem like the paragon of wisdom. They will assume you are significantly smarter than you are.

11. Initiative

When looking for people to work with, this is the first personality trait that I look for. I like to work with trigger pullers. I once knew a man who had spent three years reading books on how to talk to women but hadn't spoken to a single one. You can't learn swimming from a book either.

It's the person who reads a book and immediately leaves the house to see what will happen that achieves greatness. It's better to try and learn from experience. The people who want to know everything before they take action are cowards. They suffer from "paralysis by analysis." It's better to make a good decision now than a great decision too late.

Think about those times when you've been in a group for a conference or some team-building event. The person who speaks first usually becomes the leader. Speaking first is the only requirement to become the leader of a new group.

12. Preparation

Luck is where opportunity meets preparation. Back in my single days, I was never afraid to talk to any woman or compete with any man. Most guys start their preparation the moment they see the lady they like. My preparation started weeks earlier with choosing the perfect outfit and planning on the best ways to be charming. With my looks, I needed every advantage I could get!

Preparation is how you can defeat a foe and conquer a challenge. People naturally follow the person with the most preparation. When you go to play a round of golf, do you follow the guy who knows the lay of the land or the guy who keeps pulling a crinkled map out of his back pocket?

Whenever I want to make something happen, I spend a day in advance studying. I study the map of the airport or the list of people coming to a conference that I want to meet. Just knowing where the bathrooms are is often enough to impress people, and it gives you a chance to expand your influence.

13. Respect

Watch how someone treats waiters and bathroom attendants when nobody is looking. If they treat those people poorly, they are terrible leaders. A good leader will be loved and will lead by making the people who follow them feel respected and important. No matter how "low" the job, I have great respect for the people who perform it.

I hope I never have to work in a fast-food restaurant or in construction. Not because I think those people are dumb, but because I think they are stronger than me. I couldn't physically handle standing all day and dealing with customers like that. I have nothing but respect for people who can do a job that's hard. I respect anyone who does anything manual because I would hate to have to do that.

That level of respect will allow you to connect with people in a way that most "leaders" completely miss, and is how you can turn a competitor's staff into your greatest allies.

14. Consistent

There is nothing worse than a leader who could snap at any moment. One minute it is sunshine and daisies, and the next she is shouting your head off for a tiny mistake. That inconsistency destroys trust. If you can't trust your boss to react in a consistent manner, then you can't trust them in anything. If you are going to be a tyrant, you might as well be consistent.

15. **Organized**

This one isn't much of a surprise; it's just an extension of preparation. Imagine that you were on trial for murder and you walked into your lawyer's office. There are piles of documents everywhere and food on half of the piles. Would you be excited about your prospects or terrified?

16. **Responsive**

A good leader will listen to good advice, no matter where it comes from. It could be the little drummer boy that notices the army is about to walk into a trap. The good general heeds his warning, but the bad general will lose his entire command.

When people on your team want to share an idea, you must always listen to them. Test their ideas when you can, and if the idea is terrible, take the time to explain why. Just recently, someone came to me with an idea that I shot down immediately. He was devastated until I explained that I had the exact same idea three months earlier and I had already tested it – it was a total failure. Only because I had tried the idea already did I know it was a bomb. Once I explained that, we were able to get on the same wavelength, and now I'm testing his next idea.

17. **Resourceful**

The ultimate example of resourcefulness was the classic TV show MacGyver. Unfortunately, they have created a new, awful version of it, but the original show was about a man who could do anything with a pocket knife and some rubber bands.

A mindset change can unlock your ability to be resourceful. Just memorize this statement:

"There is no obstacle that I cannot overcome. When other people see an obstacle, that is my greatest opportunity."

This will change the way your mind thinks and keep you in a resourceful mindset.

18. Enthusiastic

Excitement is contagious. The more you believe in your product or message, the more the people around you will believe as well. You can create fanatics who simply want to follow your passion and excitement. Nobody gets excited about following a boring robot, so don't be one.

19. Adaptable

No plan survives first contact with the enemy. Whatever business you go into, however you approach life, there are going to be surprises. A good leader is able to adapt to the unforeseen and continue to thrive. Those who can't adapt fall to the wayside. Only a fool thinks that the past can predict the future. The only guarantee is that the future will surprise you. This is the joy and wonder of life, but if you're not prepared for it, it can destroy your ability to lead. The best advice I can give you is to roll with the punches.

20. Open-Minded

The only guarantee in life is that every new day will be filled with surprises. Sometimes the best ideas come from the most unexpected sources. Keep an open mind, and you might be the first person to find the next great idea.

21. Recognize Greatness

Every day in business I'm surprised. There's always somebody with a new idea or a new vision. At first, people think that idea is terrible or crazy and will never work. But then, one person believes in it, and that idea changes the world. Twelve different publishers thought that Harry Potter was garbage and rejected JK Rowling's first manuscript. Their inability to recognize greatness cost their companies billions of dollars. Something tells me that those twelve people are not in leadership positions right now.

22. Evaluation

There's a reason that this book started with an assessment. We need to know where you started in order to measure your success. A good leader is able to evaluate both himself and his followers. You must be able to recognize and reward your best workers and release those who just aren't cutting it.

Firing people is hard. It doesn't feel good, and I hate having to do it, but sometimes the best thing you can do for an inadequate employee is release them.

23. Lead by Example

This is more than just good leadership; it is also good business. When you hire someone to do a task that you cannot perform yourself or you do not understand, there is a very good chance they will rip you off. This is why ninety percent of people end up hating their contractors.

There is no task at Serve No Master that I cannot do myself. Whenever I give a task to an employee or contract worker, if they can't do it faster and better than I do it, I take over the job. Demonstrating that I know how to do something the right way is the best way to guarantee that my employees give me their best. Patton was an unbelievable general during World War II. I read his eight hundred-page biography, and one thing I learned is that he led from the front. That's why he is the only general from World War II that most people could name right now.

Reflection Questions

This book is interactive. Please grab a spiral notebook and a pen, so that you can participate in each exercise in real time. On the cover of your journal, please write "My Influence and Persuasion Journal." Then answer the following questions:

1. How much influence do you feel you have over the people in your life? Why do you feel this way?
2. If you feel you do not have a lot of influence over the people in your life, explain how that affects your leadership ability.
3. Before reading what we've learned here, did you underestimate the role of influence in leadership?
4. What do you think will be your first step towards developing a stronger level of influence? Why?
5. What do you think will be your long-term plan for developing a greater level of influence? Are you excited about the possibility of gaining more influence? Why, or why not?

Persuasion and Leadership

As a leader, no ability is more crucial than the ability to persuade. There are two ways to persuade people. You can use fancy words, or you can possess influence. The stronger your influence, the less you need to rely on fancy words to get the best from your team. Leadership, persuasion, and influence are not an art. They are a science.

As we dig further into this book, we will unlock that science. I will show you the exact system I use to build up influence and persuade people to go into business with me. If you are leading a team right now, then this book is about to change the trajectory of your career. We are going to make leadership natural. The best thing about this system is that it's enjoyable. You and the people you influence are going to enjoy every interaction from now on.

When you try to lead people without these core principles, they follow you because they have to, not because they want to. You could spend your entire life trying to motivate a donkey with a whip, but he will always resist you and try to kick you. Far better to offer him a carrot so that he wants to work with you.

Before we start the next chapter, I've got a few questions I'd like you to think about:

1. Do you already think of persuasion as a process, or have you tended to think of it as an isolated event? Did you realize that persuasion often requires planning?
2. What do you feel might be currently lacking in your persuasion skills? How do you hope to improve?
3. How do you feel that the level of your persuasion skills has affected your leadership performance in the past?

2

CREATING SHARED VALUES AND VISION

When two people meet, their worldviews collide. The worldview with the greater influence absorbs the weaker one. When you achieve this synchronicity, leadership becomes easy. People naturally follow the stronger worldview, and when you share vision and values, they become invested in your success.

Having shared values and vision will boost the effectiveness of your leadership:

- People will be much more likely to agree with you.
- People will be much more likely to want to cooperate with you.
- People will be more motivated and will want to achieve your goals as much as you do.
- People will be more willing to put in extra time and effort, and it's more likely that they will be happy to do so.
- There will be much more cohesion in the group and more open communication.
- There will not be any of the hesitation that can occur

when people don't agree or fully support what they are doing.
- People will have a fuller understanding of what they are doing, and why they are doing it.
- People will feel more fulfilled, which will result in better energy levels and work productivity.

Reflection Questions

1. Think of a time in your life when you didn't share values or vision with people you wanted to influence or persuade. What happened? Did you find it difficult to persuade them?
2. Have there been times in your life when you tried to find common ground with someone, to make them more open to your influence? This is akin to creating shared values and vision. How effective were you in doing this?
3. How important do you feel cooperation and cohesion are in today's workplace?

Exercise 1: A Leader You Admire

Choose a historical leader that you admire and would like to emulate in some way, then answer the following questions:

1. Did this leader create shared values and vision with the people they led? How did they accomplish this?
2. How did they create cooperation and cohesion within the group?
3. How did their efforts to create shared values and vision contribute to their success and to the success of their followers?

Exercise 2: Make a Plan

Before I give you all the answers, I'd like to exercise your mind a little bit. Pull out your Influence and Persuasion Journal and write down a few ways that you could create shared values and a vision for the people you wish to lead. How can you reveal your vision to them in a way that inspires them? What are some mistakes that you definitely want to avoid? Have you had a boss in the past who did this well or poorly? How can you learn from that experience?

How to Create Shared Values and Vision

There is an old saying that applies to movies and books equally, "show me, don't tell me." Nothing annoys me more than a movie with a narrator explaining all the great scenes I never got to see. I don't go to a movie to hear a narrator describe an epic battle. I want to see it in action.

The first step to creating value alignment is living the values that you espouse. One of my personal pet peeves is hypocrites. How often do you see a politician or celebrity flying on a private jet just to talk about global warming? People shouldn't drive cars, but it's ok for the rich to fly private planes? Those planes are thousands of times worse for the environment than your car will ever be. "Do as I say, not as I do." That is the worst method of leadership.

We want to follow people that believe in what they are saying. Consistency and integrity are at the core of establishing your vision. I talk about escaping the nine-to-five and taking control of your destiny in my other books. Would you listen to my message if I didn't live on a tropical island and have total control of my financial destiny? The fact that I live what I teach inspires people to come into alignment with me.

The more you believe in the product, the easier it is to sell.

Once you are living in alignment with your values, it's amazingly easy to share them. I have a friend who eats raw meat. He doesn't need to bring it up. Anyone who sees him eating immediately asks him about his values. The more you live your values, the more people will start to notice.

When you want people to follow your values, just tell them. This is why companies have mission statements. But if you're going to do that, you have to live out that statement. Your company needs to be in alignment with your vision as well.

Reflection Questions

1. How can you better share your values and vision with the world?
2. How can you ensure that your team's voices are heard when you share your vision with them? How can you make them feel appreciated, even as you bring them into alignment with your vision?
3. How is sharing values with employees different than sharing values with friends and associates? How can you ensure that your employees are on the same page as you?

3
THE ART OF PERSUASION

Persuasion is more science than art. Most people think of persuasion as a complicated craft that takes years to master – a skill that only magicians and used-cars salesmen ever truly manage to perfect.

Persuasion is far easier than this. In its most distilled form, persuasion is getting people to agree with you by telling them the right things in the right order. Most of us already know the right things to say; our challenge is saying them in the right order. That is the science of persuasion.

Persuasion is a process, but it doesn't have to take years or even days to complete. I often meet a new person and close a business deal within an hour. People wire me money after knowing me for less than sixty minutes. You've already read a few chapters of this book, so you know that I'm not very eloquent. I'm not a master orator with dulcet tones. When it comes to persuasion:

The order is far more important than the words.

The first day of training for any sales job, they teach you about "yes ladders." Get someone to say yes to something small, then something a little bigger. Keep going, and eventually they say yes to the purchase. This is a simple order of small to big yesses, but it's the perfect example of this. Get one of your questions out of order, and the entire ladder collapses.

Start the Battle First

The person who researches and prepares the most for any event, for any encounter, is the one who wins. The more knowledge you have, the easier it is to be successful and effective when you're encountering someone.

There are two big ways to research. There is general research, where you know everything about the type of crowd you're going to be interacting with and all the benefits of what you have to offer. When you know yourself well, it's easy to establish credibility; it's easy to establish expertise and demonstrate your knowledge because you researched and prepared. You can form soft connections with everyone at an event because you understand what they have in common.

Beyond that, there is a deeper level where you prepare for specific people. This is when you research someone's business model, their mindset, the way they do business, and their hobbies, so then you can then connect with them on another level. You find out that they're passionate about golf, or adult literacy, or they donate blood all the time – the things people talk about in radio interviews, newspaper articles, blog posts, and podcasts. We can find out the specific things about people and avoid making calamitous mistakes.

My friend once approached a business leader to invite him to a party we were throwing. And it severed that relationship forever.

The mistake my friend made was offering a generic connection to the one person who was the exception. Ninety-nine percent of people you can invite to an awesome party with models, booze, fun and good times, and it will work at these types of events. But he found the one person that's the exception to the rule. And this is where the specificity of your research really makes a difference.

If my friend had listened and remembered that this potential ally was married with children and did not drink, he would have talked about his impending nuptials instead. That would have given him the correct common ground.

My great success is my ability to research – the fact that I start planning my events way in advance. I only go to two events per year. That means I have to be absolutely effective in order to maintain and grow my business. Going to an event or a conference, or anytime you meet a celebrity or someone you want to do business with, you're all in. It's a really big opportunity. It can cost you a lot of money or a lot of time to travel to these events, so you want to get a big payoff. You want to get a nice return on your investment; you can't afford to spend thousands of dollars every week going to event after event until something works.

The time you spend preparing and laying out the battlefield is far more effective than the time you spend talking to people. It's what happens before and after that really makes the difference. The more you are meticulous in your preparation, the more you will know what you want, who you're going to approach, and what you're going to do. This allows you to form connections. Because you know what people like and what they're into, you can form common ground. You can develop a real rapport, so you can become the one person they remember because you're the one person they formed a real connection with.

In a way, you can think of this as either preparing the battlefield, which is where we do specific preparation for a location, or preparing to persuade, which is where we're preparing our mindset and our knowledge. These are the two practical ways we can get ready before we go to an event, before we meet anyone, before we even start the active persuasion. The person who starts the preparation first is the one who will achieve the most success.

Preparing to Persuade

There are a few key simple steps and elements to preparing to persuade, and if you take the time to implement each of these steps, you'll always be ready when you encounter that special person or when opportunity comes your way. Luck is where opportunity meets preparation, and this is the preparation we're talking about.

The first thing is to learn everything you can about your audience; the group of people you're going to be interacting with. If you're going to a conference, you want to learn what the people have in common. If you're going to a nightclub, you want to learn what brings these people together. What do they enjoy? What are their similarities? This is the first layer of research. Beyond that, when you choose specific people, you then look at their specific history and hobbies.

The second element of preparation is to study your argument and master the message you want to deliver, whether it's convincing people to work with you or to join you and form an alliance with you about a political or environmental concern. It's impossible to persuade people when they know more about your subject than you do. Depth of knowledge is just as important as charisma.

In addition to knowing all the positive elements of your position, your project, your angle, and your argument, you also need to know every single objection. Whenever you learn sales as a craft, the first thing you learn is the primary objections. There are certain objections that are just words and mean nothing, and there are certain objections that are very difficult to overcome. When you're in sales, one of the hardest objections to overcome is, "I have to ask my husband; I have to ask my wife; I'm not allowed to make financial decisions on my own." This is a hard objection, and you have to wait until the other person is present to overcome it. Most other objections you can deal with in the moment. "I'm not really sure I can afford it; I'm not ready to buy right now; I'm not sure if I want this; I don't know if I need a new car; I don't know if this meets my needs." These are soft objections where the correct response will help you to close the sale.

If you're fundraising for charity, a common objection is, "Why should I donate to you over someone else? What separates your charity from other charities?" The more you know the objections you are going to face, and the more you prepare, the easier it is to overcome them. Don't depend on yourself to think of great answers in the moment. Why work hard when you can work smart? Every argument has weaknesses. If you believe that your argument is infallible, there's a big problem. You're not seeing what other people see. I meet people all the time who have absolute faith in an argument, and they go, "I'm one hundred percent right. Everyone agrees with me." And yet, fifty or sixty percent of the population doesn't agree with them. If your argument is infallible, everyone on earth would agree with you, and yet even now, there are people who still believe the earth might be flat.

There are always people who see holes in your argument. Understanding those holes, their objections, and your biggest weaknesses and being prepared to answer them – that's the key to success. To go beyond research, especially if you're thinking about political or larger levels of influence, and you're trying to influence large groups rather than individual people, you can look at their historical actions. How did this group of people vote in the past? What are the political issues that are important to them? What do they care about? Do they care about jobs? Do they care about the environment? Do they care about crime?

Every different group has a different priority, and the main thing that the political parties do in every country is poll, poll, poll. They look at historical data. They ask questions over time. They want to find out what your most important issue is, and that's what they're going to talk about. In an area where everyone is looking for jobs, they talk about jobs. In an area where everyone is suffering from crime problems, they talk about crime. Whatever the issue is in the area, that becomes the most important part of their argument to the local audience.

Additionally, you can look for specific reasons why this person or this audience responds to this problem. If a factory just shut down in town, then everyone is going to be feeling the economy. If there was recently a major wave of crime or someone was let off on a technicality after committing some bad crimes, then that is going to be especially on their mind. When you know the specific reasons people are feeling strongly about certain issues, you can connect with them more easily.

The things that matter to me shift over time. What was important a few months ago might change when something happens in my family. If someone gets sick, suddenly healthcare becomes the most important thing. We all know cancer is a big problem, but people who have had cancer or had a family member who had cancer are far more passionate and have a much different feel about the disease than people who in general are against cancer. No one is pro-cancer, but people are on different ends of the spectrum, from, "I'm against cancer," to, "I'll do whatever it takes. I'll donate anything and donate time to fight against cancer because it affected my life." Knowing your audience and preparing this information will help you calibrate.

A final example of failure when it comes to preparing to persuade is the joke. They always teach you in traditional speech courses to start with a joke or have a joke for your audience. The danger, if you don't research your audience, is telling a joke that fails. We live in a society now where if you tell a joke that bombs or doesn't hit right or gets misinterpreted, it ends up on Twitter, and it becomes a defining moment of your life, even when people are clearly misinterpreting what you said.

People are looking for any excuse these days to value signal on Twitter and say, "Look, I found someone doing something wrong, and now I'm pointing it out to prove I'm good because they are bad." That's a big part of our culture. Failure to research is how people end up on Twitter. There are certain jokes you can tell to certain crowds. There are certain jokes that are okay in America but would get you arrested in England and vice versa. Understanding the culture and history of your people ensures that you don't tell that joke that bombs.

Establish Credibility

Nobody likes to get a message from somebody that we hate or mistrust. When I was in high school, I had a friend who was as intrigued by the concept of truth and perceptions as I am. We developed something called "reverse lie." This is where you lie all the time until a person never trusts you, and then you tell them a really important truth. The one time you tell the truth is the one time they don't believe you.

A simple example of the reverse lie is to tell a roommate that he missed a call from his parents over and over again. Every time you tell him this message, he calls his parents, and they tell him they didn't call. Eventually, he learns not to trust you and to assume that if you tell him his parents called, you're lying. So now he will no longer believe you. You've established your baseline for the reverse lie. Then his mom calls and says she needs to be picked up from the airport; you give him the message, but he won't believe you, and she ends up stranded at the airport.

What's interesting about the reverse lie is that you're doing something bad, but it gives you the moral high ground. You can say, "I didn't do anything wrong. I finally told you the truth. I told you that your mom is at the airport. You chose not to believe me."

This is a rather interesting conversational construct because it's very manipulative, and I'm pretty sure this is a concept that most politicians are very familiar with because it's a way to do something wrong and yet still manage to hold the moral high ground. It's been years since I've even thought about the reverse lie, but it highlights how important the credibility of the messenger is.

We don't like information – even if the information is correct – from someone we dislike. The way people view you as a person – your intelligence or personality, your knowledge, and your experience – all of that will color how they interpret information. A recent report came out showing that ninety-nine percent of the articles in peer-reviewed journals and inside medical journals that we all trust didn't even use the scientific method. There are massive flaws in the methodology.

It also came out recently, in another study I read, that fifty percent of those articles are put there by pharmaceutical companies because one company owns almost all of those journals, and that fake articles can get into them quite easily without ever being peer-reviewed.

And yet we trust them intrinsically because those people have extra letters after their name. Even though we know that most articles in there were either put there by a large pharmaceutical company, or the scientific method was violated, or the data wasn't peer-reviewed, you still would struggle to overcome that and distrust an article. If I mentioned the name of one of those specific journals that we all trust and I showed you an article from one of those journals, you would assume that it's correct, even with those three pieces of information I just shared with you. That's the power of credibility.

We assume in our society that all scientists are paragons of truth; that no scientist would ever lie; that no doctor would ever lie for profit. For some reason, we assume lawyers are all liars, but we assume doctors are all truth tellers, despite massive amounts of evidence the doctors and scientists are just as fallible as everyone else.

To establish maximum authority and maximum benefit when you try and influence and persuade people, you have to start with the audience's perception of your general expertise. How much do you know about the subject? How much do you know in general?

The easiest way to establish this is by having extra letters after your name. I could make you call me "Jonathan Green, MA" because I have a Master's, and I can even add "with merit," because not only did I get a Master's, I got a little bit higher level. In America, we use "cum laude" and "summa cum laude," but in England they say "with merit," and because I have an English Master's, it gets me a little more credibility. In America, we have this perception that people from England are just a little bit smarter. For some reason, the English accent to us comes across as a little smarter, so having an English set of letters after your name is even better than having American letters. This is despite the fact that a Master's program in England takes nine months as opposed to twenty-four months in America. Now you know the real reason I studied in London, but still, something about that English university sounds a little better.

Beyond trusting that you understand your subject in general, there is the level of trust your audience has in you as a professional. You're a doctor, but are you a good doctor? This is where time can really make a difference. When I was in my early twenties, one of my friends tried to get into real estate. He wanted to be a realtor, but it's very hard to get someone in their fifties to trust you when the making a million-dollar purchase. It's hard to get people to trust you as a professional when you're at the beginning of your career. Even if you might be right, that's not enough – there are other elements that come into play. This is why every university wants their professors writing and publishing as much possible. The level of trust you have in me as a professional comes from the fact that I'm a writer, an author, a published author, and then above that there is the fact that I'm a best-selling author.

Each higher level of credibility, each higher level we attain means that I can more easily get you to trust me. The more credibility you have at the beginning, the less work you have to put into the process to take people through your argument. If you already have massive amounts of credibility and expertise, then you can close a sale or win the argument in five minutes. But if they don't have a lot of trust in your credibility, you have to have a stronger, longer argument. The same sale, the same conversation can take two hours.

Beyond this, there is their trust in you as a human being. You have a great deal of expertise, you're very knowledgeable in your subject, but there's something about you that I don't trust. Most high-level investors and successful people who run businesses and make a great deal of money trust their instincts. If they have a bad feeling about someone, it is virtually impossible for that person to overcome that bad first impression. I have been on both sides of this. I have made a bad first impression before, and it's nearly impossible to overcome.

For example, if you walk up to someone directly in front of them, make full eye contact before you say the word "hello," their first second of interaction can be controlled by something inside their mind. If they are distracted and are not paying attention to what's in front of them at all, they might feel like you popped up out of nowhere, and they're going to think, "Where did you come from?" And their first emotions will be surprise, fear, and shock. It's virtually impossible to overcome. This it's not your fault; you didn't sneak up on them. They weren't looking in front of them. Their eyes were making contact with you – you just didn't realize you had their eyes turned off. And yet the exact same person, if they were paying attention and watching you, the interaction and attraction would be fine.

The way people perceive you as level-headed and in control of your emotions, objective, and reliable, is extremely important. To see a lot of these in action, you can just watch investors. I love watching shows where people with businesses or inventions seek investment. When it comes to reliability, the second someone says, "I declared bankruptcy in the past," you know they're unreliable. The odds of them getting the investment diminish. When they say, "In the past, I did something bad," or, "Someone in my family doesn't talk to me because I owe them money." They've now demonstrated that they have a pattern of unreliability or untrustworthiness.

I've also seen when someone gets very emotional – whether it's anger, passion, or sadness – they start crying, and they lose their opportunities because people who are controlled by their emotions often make poor business decisions. All of my business decisions and all my arguments are controlled by numbers. I don't make decisions about which books to write and which articles to publish based on my emotions. I write about what my audience wants. I write what will sell the most. That's the approach to business that gets investors excited. When you become emotional, people start to trust you less and less. Are you making this decision and do you believe in this argument because you believe in the numbers, or are you caught up in an emotional loop?

Communication and arguing are as much about listening as they are about talking. To influence people, they have to believe that you care what they have to say. I often meet people who have a very strong political or environmental opinion, or social causes they are passionate about. You never talk to them about it because you can never question them or ask questions. If you even asked for clarifications, "How does this work? I don't understand this logic point." They would take it personally; their reaction might be emotional or anger, or they'd shut you down. "How dare you question my argument?" Not only is it emotional, but they're also demonstrating bad conversational skills because they're not listening.

I would never work with an intern who is not teachable; who doesn't listen; who doesn't respond to what I say and try to improve. No one wants to mentor people who are not teachable. No one wants to work with people who don't listen. Someone can believe in your argument and want to be in alignment with your opinion, but not with you, because you don't listen, and they don't feel like you give their voice significance. There are many people – often the people who are most passionate about something – who love the sound of their own voice. And the louder they shout, the less other people listen.

The final way to establish credibility with your audience is to demonstrate that you're looking out for their best interests. For every argument, for every political opinion, for everything you want to do, every way you want to persuade or convince people, you can focus on the benefits for yourself, or you can focus on the benefits for them. "If you elect me, I'll bring more jobs to your community which will lower crime, which means you will feel safer in your home." Everyone's favorite subject is themselves. When you make your argument about improving their lives, that's when you do really well.

In sales letters, we call this "focusing on the benefits." What's the benefit to the reader? What's the benefit to the customer? How will this product help them? In the same way that you read the description of this book, all the first elements were how this book can help you become more influential and more persuasive, and how those elements can help you have a better life; how you can get more promotions; get more investment for your businesses; get people to trust you more; form stronger and better business alliances. All of these things are the benefits to you from reading this book.

Perception

What you say isn't nearly as important as what your audience hears. This applies to both the present and the past. If you ask two people at the same incident, you will often get a conflicting report. Eyewitness testimony is notoriously unreliable for this reason. Recently, there was an argument online about whether a particular dress was blue or gold, and people were shouting at each other, calling each other colorblind, and they were throwing out pretty harsh words because if anything is objective, it's surely color. The sky is blue, right? If I say the sky is blue and someone else says it's gold, there must be something wrong with that person.

But it turns out that the argument was not about color but math, and that based on the way you perceive certain numbers, the ratio of the receptors in your eyes determined whether you saw blue or gold. Different segments of the population really did see two different colors. They were both objectively correct, and to each person, their perception is more important than anything else.

Emotion and perception are very important parts of the persuasion process. When you connect with someone on an emotional level, and you know the way to approach them based on your research, you're halfway there. Understanding the way people see the universe and their most important issues allows you to connect with them in a powerful and dynamic way. There are a few key elements of perception you want to keep in mind as you approach people. The first that we've already hinted at is that you shouldn't assume that just because something is true, other people agree with it or perceive it the same way.

Oftentimes, there are things that you believe are unequivocally true. You can one hundred percent believe in something, and yet someone else one hundred percent does not. And when you rely on that as one of the steps in your argument, you lose them. There are people that positively believe that global warming is the most important environmental disaster, and the most important human issue affecting us in the history of our planet, and they absolutely believe in global warming as a fact. And yet, there are just as many people (if not more) who believe that global warming is one hundred percent false.

If you read Serve No Master, you will remember that I talked about the very first scientist who wrote a book about global warming. Ten years earlier, he had also written a book about global cooling. This is perfect example of me checking out the credibility of someone before I listen to their arguments. I'm not trying to get you to follow either side of the argument. What I want you to understand is that people on each side of that argument perceive a different set of facts. When someone starts with a different set of perceptions, you may have to begin your story or your argument earlier down the chain. Instead of starting at step three, you have to go back and start at step one, and that's okay.

You always must demonstrate that you respect other people's viewpoints, or you will lose them instantly. The reason I mention global warming is because people are so firmly on one side or the other that they no longer listen to arguments. Whenever I bring up certain pieces of scientific data, most people on one side or the other have no idea what I'm talking about, and that's a problem. If you only listen to people who agree with you, if you only understand your side of the perception, then you're caught in groupthink, and you won't be able to affect people on the other side of the aisle.

Why do you think almost every issue is split fifty/fifty? Once people choose a side to get locked in, once you declare a political party in our society, you subtly have to agree with every platform and every decision that political party makes, and it's very adversarial. I'm A; you're B. We're opposites; we could never get along. We have to disagree on everything. We're constantly seeking difference as opposed to seeking rapport.

When you talk to someone and they can tell that you don't respect their opinion, they will stop listening to you. Would you listen to someone who did not respect you, even if they were right? With every single point in this book, just ask yourself if you are the receiver rather than the arguer. How would you respond to someone who thought you were an idiot and wanted to convince you of something else? The moment you notice they thought you're an idiot, you would stop listening to them because it became personal.

You want to make sure and demonstrate that you are aware of all sides of the argument. You can talk about both sides of global warming, talk about different aspects of the argument and different pieces of data that disagree with each other – two sets of historical data. There are several pieces of data that were found to be false. Some data turned out to be falsified, and the scientists in charge of that data decided to delete it, despite it being against the law to delete cooling and warming data, and earth temperature data. These scientists deleted it and said, "Whoops! But trust us!"

Would you trust someone who deleted data? I wouldn't. It doesn't matter what their argument is; anyone who deletes the data, I don't trust. And yet, people who are in alignment with their opinion don't care that they deleted the data. They say, "Oh, it was probably just an accident," and the people on the other side of the argument say, "No, if you delete the data, it had to be on purpose."

We let our political opinions affect us first. I find it very interesting that the people who often talk about global warming talk about a lot of mechanical problems, but they never talk about overpopulation. It's interesting because it's the same people who used to make different arguments.

When someone doesn't know every aspect of an argument – when they don't know the pros and the cons – their credibility diminishes. Don't pretend that there aren't people who disagree with you; don't pretend you aren't aware of it.

Most people only get the news from whichever side of the aisle they sit in. Therefore, they only hear news they agree with. This means they often make arguments and have opinions without all the information. Even if you were to watch all the different news channels, it's very hard to get reality anymore, because entertainment, ratings, and opinions have colored everything so much that there is no objective news anymore. There is no such thing as the trusted anchor, like we used to have in the fifties and sixties. That era is over, but the more you understand the totality of an argument, the more credibility you have.

You should actively show yourself to be a good listener. Let other people speak first. Whenever I want to convince someone of an opinion, I want them to speak first. If I want to form an alliance with someone, the more they speak first, the better. When they speak first, they trust me more, they like me more, and they are giving me free data. All that research we were just talking about, they are giving it to you in the moment. They're saying, "Maybe you haven't researched it yet, but here's how I feel about A, B, and C." When you know their opinions, you can then adjust your argument and the way you influence, and customize it just to them, because you're actively listening.

When working with a team or forming alliances, demonstrate that you care about the success of each team member; that you are aware of each person's weaknesses and strengths. One of the easiest ways for me to form alliances is to point out my strengths and weaknesses right out of the gate. When I first became a writer, I would often tell people that I can write an amazing book, but I'm terrible at copywriting and chapter titles. Those were my weaknesses. And for anyone good at copy, those are easy to handle. They go, "Great; we can form a great alliance because your weaknesses are my strengths." People want to work with you when they are strong where you are weak, and weak where you are strong. That's where you find the best alliances. That's where the gold is. Remember: what you say isn't nearly as important as what they hear. Nothing is objective anymore. It's what they hear and what they interpret that truly affects how they make decisions.

Reflection Questions

Like with all other reflection questions and exercises in this book, you should record your answers in your Influence and Persuasion Journal.

1. How strong or weak do you feel your persuasion skills and

practices have been up to this point? How do you feel you could improve?
2. How much new insight into persuasion have you obtained through reading this chapter? How and when do you plan to put this new insight to use?

Exercise 1: Persuasion in Everyday Life

The next time you're thinking about persuading someone, no matter how big or small the issue, reflect and use as many of the techniques from this chapter as you can remember. When you want to convince your husband or wife or your friends about which movie to see this weekend, rather than focusing on why you want to see it, focus on the benefits for them. Focus on the parts they'll enjoy. You'll find it's easier to get people to go along with you, and in fact, you will both enjoy the experience a little bit more.

This exercise doesn't need to start with career decisions, work decisions, or anything big. We can start with small things just to experiment. When I'm choosing a movie to watch with my wife, because I know her history and the movies that she likes, I know how to talk her into seeing a different movie. The good thing is she enjoys the experience of going to a movie so much that it almost doesn't matter what's happening in the movie, and because I understand that I focus on the experience.

When I took her to a movie last week, I said, "Let me take you to a movie. We're going to make it a whole big event. We're getting dressed up. We're going to leave a little bit early. We're going to get food from somewhere other than the movie theater (where we go to the movies you are allowed to choose from several different restaurants – you don't have to get popcorn). We're going to get drinks at one place, we're going to get snacks from somewhere else, and we're going to have a whole experience." When I'm inviting her to a movie, I focus on the part I know she enjoys the most: the experience, rather than the story and the movie itself.

It's very important, when you're implementing the lessons from this chapter, that you believe in what you're trying to do. Don't convince someone to see a movie you don't want to see because then you are going to end up seeing a movie you don't want to see. I want to warn you that random practice does not make perfect; only practice persuading people with things you absolutely believe in does. Learning to persuade people of things you don't believe in will mess up the way you express yourself and actually cause more problems down the line.

I recommend you try this exercise three or four times this week. It's amazing how often persuasion can come up: deciding where to go to lunch; deciding which project to work on first; deciding what movie to watch. There are so many different places where we make decisions cooperatively.

After you've convinced someone, ask them about the conversation. Say, "Hey, do you feel like I'm a little bit more persuasive this week than I was last week? How do you feel about how we chose to watch a movie?" Get a little feedback from them. Remember, we're not learning to manipulate. We're learning to give people what they want in a more effective manner. Ask them how effective they thought your effort to persuade them was. Maybe your efforts will fail, and you end up going to the wrong movie; the movie you didn't want to see anyways. Great, but still ask about it. "Why did I end up losing this argument? Why did my persuasion efforts fail?" We can learn more from our failures than from our successes.

As a mental exercise, you can write out some imaginary conversations and practice some of these scenarios in your journal. You can pretend that you're an office manager trying to persuade workers to take a certain position; trying to convince your workers to take a pay cut or to work on a Saturday. Write down in your Influence and Persuasion Journal a couple of different plans and what you would do in each of these different scenarios.:

1. What are you going to do when you try to convince the workers to work a couple of extra hours?

2. What do you do when you want to convince your workers to cancel the office Christmas party?
3. Come up with some of your own ideas. Put a little bit of creativity in this. You know more about your business than I do.

4

CREATION OF A POSITIVE WORKPLACE CULTURE

If you're not actively creating and shaping the culture of your workplace, then someone else is. Company culture can sometimes seem rather vague, and we often think of company culture as businesses in Silicon Valley that define company culture by wearing hoodies and jeans and flip-flops rather than suits and ties; by playing ping-pong and eating together; providing free buses to work. But company culture is about so much more than that. As a leader, it's important to create a positive and functional workplace culture – a place where people feel safe expressing themselves and are driven to give their best. The creation and fostering of a positive and productive workplace culture is the hallmark of an effective leader.

Exercise 1: Brainstorming

Let's take a moment to work together actively. Let's brainstorm and think: what does company culture or workplace culture mean to you? How do you define it? Do you define it by the way people in the office dress or spend time together? Could it be how people go to and from work? Or is there more to it than that?

What are the positive aspects of a company's culture? What are the negative aspects that could bring it crashing down?

When thinking about company culture, we want to focus on activities exercises, techniques, elements that will improve employee morale and productivity; we always want to think about our purpose or our goal. The purpose of company culture is to create happier and more effective employees, and morale and productivity are the easiest ways to measure that.

How to Promote a Positive Workplace Culture

There are several key elements and components of a good workplace culture that will make people want to work with you and stay in alliance with you, and will help you to get the best out of them.

The first of those is having clear, effective, and open lines of communication. A good leader listens to the ideas of their workers. Oftentimes, it's the boots on the ground that come up with the most creative, innovative and brilliant ideas. I frequently get emails from members of my tribe – people who have read one of my books – and they question something I said, or they have a different opinion, or they ask me something poignant. When my first reaction is annoyance – when I go, "How dare you question that?" – I often need to check that emotion, because that happens when people have the best and most brilliant questions.

It's the questions about core concepts that really challenge me that often lead to moments of brilliance. Some of the greatest materials I've ever taught and some of my greatest business innovations came from the most unexpected places. If you don't listen to your employees, if you make them feel like their job is to be seen and not heard, they will take those brilliant ideas elsewhere. They will stop giving you their best.

Number two: demonstrate that you care about people both as employees and as human beings. Do you know your employees' birthdays? Do you know what matters to them? Do know their children's names? Do you know why they work for you? Do you know how they entered this business? Do you know their hopes and dreams? People will often work for less money when they are working for a company and a boss that makes them feel heard and cared about. You can often get more from someone with a present than from giving them a raise of equivalent value. People want to feel special; that's why a present means so much more than a gift card.

Encourage employees to provide feedback – you want to hear what they think about your ideas, about your content, about where the business is going. Oftentimes, they'll notice things before you do. When you're leading a team at the top, and there's a tremor at the bottom, that little tremor travels through the team, and it can get quite large before it reaches you. But if your people feel comfortable giving you feedback early on, then you can catch problems before they become big problems.

Demonstrate that you appreciate people. When people give you feedback or point out things, let them know you appreciate it. I get emails all the time where people notice mistakes on my website, in my membership area, in my blog posts, in my Facebook posts, in my books. Sometimes someone will email me, and I'm shocked to discover that a link has been broken for a year and no one else has told me.

I built most of my website myself. I don't have a huge tech team that does all the website building and those elements. I write my own books. I connect all my blog posts together and put together my podcast episodes. That critical feedback helped me make the experience better for everyone else. Yes, I'm annoyed that it's been broken for a year and no one's noticed, but I'm excited to know that no one will ever have to face this problem again; it's now been fixed.

When people send me criticism and negative feedback about something broken or a mistake I made or something they disagree with, it helps me provide something better for everyone in the future, so I always say, "Thank you for pointing that out to me; that really helps me," and I often send them something else to look at and ask if they are willing to look at one of my courses or one of the other books. That's how I show that I appreciate people giving feedback.

It's important to be collaborative when you're establishing your workplace values and vision. Yes, you're the captain, but if you establish a set of values that are too far different from what everyone else on your team believes, they won't be able to come into alignment with you. If you have a small team or you're just starting out, or even if you have been going down this path for a while, it's worth having a meeting and saying, "Guys, what do you think the vision for this company is?" If you haven't established a vision, then you'll discover each person has their own. Each person sees the company going somewhere different. And this can be why the people you're leading are often going in different directions than you – because they don't hear the same mission.

Two people can be walking down the road side-by-side, but if they're on two different missions, the way they treat everything will be very different. This is why you want to create a collaborative vision and work with people, see where they're coming from, and establish a vision that is in alignment with what you want but is also something that they can feel pulled into. You want to be very clear about expectations. Whether you're working with clients or with a team, expectation management is critical. If someone thinks a project is going to take seven days but it's going to take sixty, on day eight, it's going to be real rough. It's much better to manage expectations early on and clearly explain to people what you expect from them. There is nothing worse for an employee than working for a boss who doesn't define what they're supposed to be doing.

For everyone who works for me, I have a clear definition of what I expect them to deliver. Every single person who works for me sends me an email every Friday with a report of what they accomplished that week. It takes them maybe five or ten minutes to write the email, but it allows me to see where they are and make sure we both understand what they're supposed to be accomplishing. And for different tasks, I have different metrics. You can't measure every job in the same way. For my transcriptionist, her work is measured by how many hours she transcribed. For my assistant who does research for me, how many projects she completed and how much data she put together. And for my social media manager, we look more at successes: how many new followers do I have on Instagram? How many retweets did I get? Are things trending? We look at a bunch of graphs, because there's tons and tons of data available for social media, and she explains them to me.

Each person knows their expectations, and they know how I measure their work, and because we check that measurement once a week, they never have to worry that they're getting too far off-track. There's nothing worse than wondering if you been off-track for four weeks. You start to feel more distance from your work, and your efforts will diminish. This is why we want to be very clear with our expectations from our team, so they can know if they're meeting them.

You want to demonstrate transparency in your decision-making process and in how you evaluate people's work. If someone is not living up to your expectations and they don't know it, you're eventually going to fire them, and they can be very confused about why; it's going to become a very negative emotional experience. But if you communicate with them every week and tell them your expectation, and then point out whether they hit or fail to hit your expectation point, it's very easy to go down that path. I had to let someone go last year. Her job was very specific. She was supposed to do a certain number of tasks every week, and she never hit her number. Every week, I would say, "You didn't hit your number. You didn't hit your number," and yet when I let her go, she was shocked. And I said, "You've never hit your number." Because I was transparent from the beginning, I felt very comfortable cutting the cord. I probably kept her on the team for too long. She knew what her number was. She didn't hit it. There shouldn't be any confusion.

Because you're transparent in your decision-making, because you're transparent in your evaluation, and because you communicate with your team on a regular basis, it's very easy for everyone to know exactly where they stand. There's no confusion. There's no worry that they're off-track. You want to emphasize accountability. When someone's in charge of something and they make a mistake, you need to point out that it was their mistake, but you should also remember that you're the boss. The buck stops with you. When something goes wrong inside my team or on one of my projects, and something slips through the cracks because I didn't check it – someone makes a mistake and I didn't check it – there are two problems. The first is that the person made a mistake and the second is that I didn't catch it. There's accountability in both places. I'm accountable for everything that goes in and out of this business. If something slips through the cracks or there's a glitch, I carry that burden. I have a level of responsibility and a level of accountability.

If you're someone who always blames your employees or always wants to blame someone else, or always explains how it's anyone's fault except your own, that does not engender a good workplace culture. You want to demonstrate clear communication, clear expression of vision, and consistency with that. You cannot give someone a task and then change it every week. Pivoting your business, pivoting your business model, and pivoting your vision every week means that people can't keep up with you. They're spending half the time trying to figure out what they're supposed to be doing rather than actually doing it.

We've all had jobs where our bosses were inconsistent and unclear about what we were supposed to be doing. One week you can do a task. The next week you do the same thing, and you get in trouble for it. "No, you're supposed to be doing something different this week." One week your boss is very friendly; the next week your boss is very stern. This is a very tough area. I've made this mistake myself as a boss.

For a while, my mindset was that we're all a family at my company; everyone who works for me is a family; we're going to be really close and know everything about each other. And then, when it came time to be the boss, I started noticing that people weren't working hard because the family thing wasn't working. I had to start letting people go. I couldn't shift to being strict. I had to start over with new people. This is something that you go through when you start hiring your first employees. If you make the same mistakes I initially did, you'll have to recalibrate, and sometimes with a relationship it's too hard, and you have to start over. You have to be consistent, and it's better to start off on the right foot.

Why is a Positive Workplace Culture Important?

We've talked about how to develop and create a positive workplace culture, but perhaps you're unsure of why it's important. It creates an environment where your employees do better work, they're more satisfied, and in the long run, they put in more hours and more effort, meaning you get more value for every dollar you are paying in salary. In addition, when there's a positive workplace culture, when people feel heard and accepted and are in line with your vision, they are less likely to leave your company. Your employees last longer, and you spend less time trying to adapt to lost employees or having other people cover their work, or trying to hire new people and investing time in going through the entire recruitment and training process. Your employees are going to be happier and more satisfied with their lives. They're going to feel a sense of commitment, and they're going to want to work as hard as they can.

Workplace culture is the real driving force behind a great team's motivation. You employees will feel more pride in their workplace, and they will also communicate with each other better. We've all heard stories about different federal departments not communicating with each other. And because of this, there are massive problems. You don't want that within your company. The more people communicate with each other, the more they feel safe communicating, the more they feel heard, the more small problems never become big problems.

The final and most important reason is that your employees will feel the freedom to perform their jobs to the best of their abilities and they won't be distracted by all these other things. They won't be distracted by office politics, or worrying about their job, or worrying about whether they're doing things wrong, or wondering if they're in alignment with your vision. This clarity of vision and a healthy workplace environment allow them to focus on what you pay them for.

5

TEAM DYNAMICS

Team or group dynamics are an extremely important responsibility, and the leader is responsible for the way people interact and communicate with each other. If the leader fails to construct or promote positive group dynamics, this can lead to larger problems – this is where cracks can form within your team. As the leader, you need to pay attention to how your team interacts not only with you, but also with each other.

This starts by knowing each team member's strengths and weaknesses, so you know who will work well together and who won't. Sometimes, we are tempted to put together our two best workers to form a team, and they will do a great job. Our third and fourth best workers working together won't necessarily do that well. You get better overall performance by combining team members one and four and team members two and three. As leaders, we need to look at the totality of our results; look at where everything goes. When a group has good dynamics, the members will trust each other, they will be fair with one another, and they will hold each other accountable.

A sign that there are problems in group dynamics is blaming and passing the buck. Bad group dynamics are characterized by people stealing credit from each other and then, when something doesn't go right, they immediately blame each other. This is a sign that they don't feel the cohesiveness of alliance – they don't feel like a team. A good team can make collective decisions effectively – they can make them quickly without anyone's feeling getting hurt.

I will never forget about fifteen years ago; I was in Europe as a volunteer, and I was in a meeting deciding what game we were going to play the next day. We had an eight-hour meeting to determine a game we were going to play for ninety seconds. Though most of the group liked each other, this is a sign of a very ineffective team, which as a collection had accomplished very little. Everyone had their own set of goals; everyone pushed what they thought was the best game. Even when I said, "Let's just chose one, come on, we are wasting time!" That was rejected because other people felt that there were different goals more important than getting a job done on time. When you have five, six or eight people who are all after a different goal, you can't have an effective meeting about what your goal is – let alone accomplishing something.

Groups with good dynamics also show a great deal of creativity. People are more comfortable expressing their ideas and brainstorming. We have all been in the classroom in high school or college where the teacher tries to start a brainstorming session, and no one wants to go first; no one raises their hands because the first person to raise their hand is perceived as the teacher's pet, so there are negative social consequences for joining the teacher's activity. We want the opposite in our work environment; we want our teams to feel comfortable bringing us terrible ideas. It doesn't matter how bad the idea is; they will still build up to moments of brilliance, and we will never get to those moments of brilliance if people are never allowed to express those bad ideas.

Oftentimes, my team will bring me ideas that I know are bad because I have already tested them. Recently, a team member had an idea that she wanted to try, and on paper it sounded brilliant. Unfortunately, it is a terrible idea – I know this because I had the idea six months before, I tried it, and it failed. "I wouldn't know your idea wouldn't work except for I have tested it." I wanted to encourage her to understand that she was on the right path because we were in alignment with our ideas, but unfortunately, this particular one didn't work when I tried it.

When there are bad group dynamics, people are jockeying for position or leadership approval; they are in competition with each other. Communication suffers, people don't share their ideas, people are whispering to each other and have little ideas in their little cliques – they don't contribute everything to the center or overall discussion. Having been a teacher for more than ten years, I can remember time after time when my class started doing this; it is an absolute nightmare! You want your team to work together and feel comfortable enough to share every idea with the group.

You also have to watch out for individuals who are just trying to skate by and live off other people's work. We have all been in a situation where one person worked hard and another didn't, and the boss who was too distant, or the middle manager who wasn't paying enough attention, acted like the two people worked equally. When one person does ninety percent of the work and the other does ten percent, but they each get fifty percent of the credit, you are planting a seed for bitterness.

The better employee, the one that worked harder, will become bitter and will eventually say something.

The ignorant boss or the bad leader will then punish the worker for pointing out this other person because we have this mindset that nobody likes a tattletale. So we punish the person ratting out the other employee even though the problem didn't start between the two employees. The problem started with a bad leader who wasn't paying enough attention to who was working hard and who wasn't; a bad leader who gave inappropriate credit.

It is interesting to watch a bad leader find a way to embitter and eventually have to fire the better worker, and after several of these decisions be left with ten percenters only. They are left with a group of employees whose combined efforts aren't worth one of the employees they have gotten rid of because of their bitterness. This is why we want to watch for team dynamics earlier.

In order to ensure you are not one of these bad leaders, there are a few simple actions you can take. Start by clearly defining each individual's role as well as the role of each team and the role of the company as well. We have already discussed this a little bit by explaining to people what their jobs are, what you expect of them, and explaining your company vision, but we also want them to see what their jobs are in relation to other people.

Sometimes a new employee enters a company, has their job description and thinks, "This is what I am supposed to be doing." But one of your employees who has been there longer, one of your ten percenters will say, "Hey, I need you to work on this."

The new employee will go, "It's not in my job description."

"Well, yeah, but this is what the last person who had your job did, this is your job," and they will start to pass work onto the new employee.

Then the new employee finishes the work and gives it to the other employee who hands it in to you, and you don't notice it. You don't want that to happen; you want to watch out for people taking advantage of new employees or passing their labor onto other people. You need to clearly define who is in charge of each different kind of task.

It is tempting to give extra work to one of your employees. When a person is really good in one area, sometimes you want to expand their responsibility into another area, but you move them out of their area of expertise. It's very tempting for me to send other assignments to my transcriptionist; she is a great writer, she is fast, and there would be a lot of other types of things I could have her working on, but she is a phenomenal transcriptionist. In the transcription department, she is as close to one hundred percent of a worker than I have ever dealt with. So if I brought her to work in editing, or writing, or something else where she is at ninety percent, she would be working at ten percent below her usual efficiency, and the same thing comes with ideas for my social media person or working with my assistant or my head researcher.

When you give people extra tasks that start mingling with other people's departments, you might be rewarding good behavior, but when you are going outside of their job, you can begin to create problems.

If you are going to give someone a new responsibility, you have to redefine their new job role. This may mean you have to bring in a pay rise, you have to change their relationship with other people, and give them a positional title change. You need to be very serious when you consider these types of decisions. Asking someone to take on an extra task doesn't seem like a big deal, but if it means you have to rethink what you pay them, their hours, and their job title, you will take it more seriously. This means you will be less likely to slip up and create fractures within your team.

Do everything in your power to encourage clear, comfortable and open communication, where people can tell you on day one of a new problem. And as soon as you start to hear a glimmer, a tiny spark of a problem, you have to deal with it as the leader. The leader of a team has to take quick action.

Whenever I notice a problem within my business, the longer I take to deal with it, the bigger the problem becomes. Sometimes, when you have a problem, you go, "I don't want to deal with this right now," and you bury your head in the sand, but the problem only gets worse. Sometimes, you have a problem and you can fix it with a tiny conversation on day one, but in two weeks you have to fire someone.

Problems can grow into monsters. Always pay attention to how your team is interacting with you and with each other, and the quality of their work. Whenever you notice something slipping, start to communicate with them and find out exactly what is going on. This will ensure you have powerful and healthy team dynamics.

Reflection Questions

1. In any area of your life, including the workplace or school, have you ever experienced being in a group with poor and unproductive group dynamics? What did you feel caused

those poor dynamics at the time? Do you have different opinions on what may have caused the poor dynamics now?
2. As a leader, what will you do in the future to ensure that the people you are leading will maintain positive group dynamics? How will you improve your past performance?
3. Reflect on the connection between effective influence and strong team dynamics.
4. Reflect on the connection between effective persuasion and team dynamics.
5. Imagine you are the leader of a team that you see has negative dynamics. What steps would you take to try to improve the dynamics of the team?

6

COMMUNICATION

It almost goes without saying that strong communication skills are a critical element of this entire process. In order to influence, persuade or lead, you need to be able to express your ideas, visions, and argument. We have a tendency to believe our communication skills are better than they are, and we often give ourselves more credit than we deserve. Perhaps you have even met someone who talks about how they are a great communicator or a great salesman, but then when you ask them to demonstrate this skill, you notice they aren't nearly as good as they think they are.

No matter where you are on the spectrum; whether you are the worst communicator or the best, you can still improve! There are always new techniques, methods, and manners in which you can improve yourself and become a more effective communicator, and thus a better influencer.

There are four main areas of communication: speaking, listening, writing, and reading. We have our verbal communication, which is sending and receiving messages, and non-verbal communication, sending and receiving messages. All four of these are very important. Most people focus just on writing or just on speaking, to the detriment of their listening and reading skills. For a long time, my strength in persuasion was only verbal; when it came to written persuasion, I was awful. Being good at one did not make me good at the other, and it took me years to overcome the disparity and bring my written communication skills to the same level.

Wherever you are strong, you will have a tendency to rely on that ability; if you are a good speaker, you won't do much reading and writing; if you are a good writer, maybe you didn't do as much listening. You want to be strong in all four areas – you want to be an ambidextrous communicator.

Listening Skills

Listening is a critical component in being a good communicator – one of the best measurements of the success of a relationship, marriage, or a couple is if each partner feels like their voice is heard. It does not matter if their voice is actually heard, it only matters that they *feel* like they are being heard. Perception is everything when you are communicating with someone. Even if your message is amazing, if they feel like you are ignoring their responses, your persuasion becomes irrelevant.

About once a week, I get added on Skype by a robot. Sometimes the name looks a little bit familiar, and I will accept the invitation and say, "Hey, are you someone I know? Are you a client, reader, fan, friend of a friend, or someone I met at an event?" They immediately go into a set of automated responses, usually saying, "I'm a woman, I'm this old, and I found you in the member directory."

I don't know if Skype even has a member directory – I don't think it does – but I certainly don't have any public information there. This is how you can tell you are talking to a robot – this is how an artificial intelligence fails the Turing test. The inability to convince another person that it is human. It lacks the ability to listen.

If your responses are not reacting to what the other person says, you are failing the Turing test, and you will lose engagement. They will respond to you the same way I respond to these robots that add me and try to sell me who knows what: I block them and report them to Skype, so they get deleted and banned.

We want to do more than just hear what other people say; we want to actively listen. That means that you take the information that they give you, you absorb it into your brain, and it affects what you say next to them. This is called active listening. It is the practice of consciously listening to everything someone says and mentally engaging with the content – actually engaging with what they are saying. Many people are just on pause when you are speaking; they are just listening to the sounds of your voice and waiting for their turn to speak. This is not active listening.

A way to demonstrate active listening is to mirror the other person's phrasing and to reflect the way that they speak. Most people communicate using one of their senses. They say "feel" or they use their ears, their nose, or their mouth. They say, "This smells like trouble," or, "This sounds like a bad idea." Whichever sense they communicate in, you want to respond in the same sense. If someone talks about feeling, you talk about feel. If they talk about smell, you talk about smell, and the same with sound, and even taste: "I don't like the taste of this idea." "I don't like the taste of this idea either." This is how you can get into rapport with someone because you are communicating with them in the same way that they communicate; you are now speaking their language.

A classic example of this technique is what psychiatrists do. You sit on the psychiatrist's chair, and you speak for twenty minutes, whether they are listening or not. Sometimes they are writing notes and, as soon as you stop, they will repeat the last few words you said and make it sound like a question. You finish a story, and the last word you say is "mother;" they will repeat it with a rising intonation – the sign of a question. It is a way to get you to continue speaking and feel like they are actively listening. You can use this same technique, repeat back the last few words of what the person said to you, and it will feel like you are actively listening, and communication will continue.

People appreciate it when they feel like you are listening to them.

This is often how politicians become successful; it's not that they actively listen to their constituents, but their constituents feel like they are heard. Truly successful politicians hide their ego when they are meeting with the voters. They make them feel like they are important, even though we all know later on the politician will ignore everything the voters asked for and do whatever they feel like.

When people feel heard, they are more likely to come into alignment with you; they are more likely to enjoy being a part of your team. They are going to put in more effort, and they are going to become a big scorer of all of your ideas. They will feel like they are truly a member of your team, and that you listen to their ideas and take them into account as you make team decisions, so even if you make a decision that goes against your original ideas, as long as they feel heard, they will come into alignment with your leadership.

Active Listening Exercise

The next time you are listening to someone and they express a thought or an idea, I want you to practice active listening. Pay attention to what they are saying, and modify your responses based on what they say. At the very least, use the psychiatrist technique and repeat their last word to them in the form of a question. After you have gone through this activity, I want you to write down the answers to the following questions in your Influence and Persuasion Journal.

1. How do you feel that your practice in active listening has improved your connection or rapport with the other person?
2. Do you think that the other person noticed that you were listening more attentively? Do you think they appreciated it? How did they express their appreciation? How did they communicate differently?
3. Do you feel like this conversation was better than other conversations you have had with them in the past? Did it feel like the overall conversation was of a higher quality?

4. Are you surprised by your results? Were you surprised that active listening led to better communication? Are you excited about trying active listening more and watching how it increases your ability to influence people in both your professional and personal life?

Speaking Skills

One of the most common fears in our society is the fear of public speaking. If you feel uncomfortable and overwhelmed by the idea of speaking in public, you are not alone. Everyone is afraid of public speaking in one way or another. Some people are fine speaking to a crowd of three or four thousand people, but with three or four people they get uncomfortable. For some people, it is the opposite – small crowds are fine, big crowds are horrifying.

My fear of public speaking manifests itself in the form of poetry. There is nothing that I despise and dread more than having to read a poem in public. Whenever I had to recite a poem in high school, my heart would be racing, terrified of the process. No matter how much I practiced repeating my poem at home, when I got up in front of the classroom, I would be sweating bullets. That is my public speaking nightmare.

Whether you are speaking to one person, a small group, or the masses, there are a few techniques you can use to improve your speaking skills.

1. Focus on clarity of both message and communication. Some great authors have a tendency to use big words that their audience doesn't understand. If you go to England and use American slang, the audience won't understand you. If you mumble or speak too quietly, the audience will struggle to hear you. This is a very common problem for nervous public speakers; speaking quietly makes the problem worse, and you create a self-fulfilling prophecy.

2. Prepare everything you need to say in advance, or at least make sure you have an outline in your mind of what you are going to talk about, so you have a solid structure. It is very easy when you are in

the middle of a talk, speech, or argument to stop on one of your points and forget what was coming next. You end up going down this rabbit hole and start losing focus, and even though the person was engaged, as you get distracted they get more distracted as well. Try not to jump from topic to topic; focus one argument until it is completed and then move on to the next one.

3. Confidence. If you don't believe in the product, no one else will. When you are speaking, influencing, or arguing, you as a person are the product. The more you believe in yourself, the more people will believe in you. This leads to a bit of a catch-22, "I can't speak well unless I am confident." "I can't be confident if I don't speak well." The best method is to fake it until you make it.

Imagine you are a more confident person or create a character that is the confident version of you. My character is Confident Jonathan, and I say, "What would Confident Jonathan do or say in this situation?" As soon as you add this one layer between you and your behavior, where you pretend that you are someone more confident, you will come across as more confident because you are behaving more confident.

4. Cohesiveness. Look at your argument and remove any extraneous elements. As a writer, I find it very easy to print massive amounts of content. My challenge is going through them and slashing all the unnecessary parts. What you want is to say the bare minimum to get your point across – there is no reason to waste someone else's time once they agree with you.

5. An open and friendly demeanor. Your body language should express openness and show that you are willing to listen. If you cross your arms and have a frown on your face, people will feel uncomfortable listening to you, as you are expressing intimidation rather than friendliness. People listen to people that they trust and like.

6. Ask questions. Even when speaking to a large group, you can ask questions and get the audience and respond to you. "Stand up if you believe Y." "Stand up if you agree with X." When speaking online using a webinar, or using anything involving technology, it is easy to add a poll or survey where everyone can answer what they want. The

more you communicate with your audience, the more they will feel heard, and the more you can design your speech and modify it on the fly to match what they want. Sometimes, you'll ask a question and discover that people are on a completely different page than you thought; all of your research was wrong and you need to modify your talk. Thank goodness you asked that question so that you can respond and give a better talk based on their actual needs.

7. Contextual awareness. Be aware of your audience's background, their geographic location, their experience, knowledge, and all of the things they bring to the table. I sometimes see speakers using quotes, and they don't know who they are from. A perfect example of this is the quote, "We must tear asunder the past before we can truly create the future." Sounds pretty great as a motivational quote, and I have seen people use that quote without knowing that the original speaker is Hitler. Please do your research before you quote someone. If you accidentally quote a villain, it's not going to help you win your argument when someone in the audience knows.

8. Situational Awareness. Be aware of what is happening in the room. Are people leaving the room, are people crying, are they responding emotionally? I once went to see a speaker who wrote a book on the art of conversation. She sat down in front of a room with about thirty people and read the entire speech from her notebook without looking up once. She never spoke to the audience, and her book was about conversation. Needless to say, everyone left the room feeling disappointed. Pay attention to how your audience is responding; the more it feels like a conversation, the stronger your leadership will be.

9. Understanding and paying attention to the body language of your listeners. The way people sit, move, fidget, and act tells you everything you need to know. As a teacher, I have been there where everyone in the class starts falling asleep. Sometimes, as a teacher, you are trapped by limitations, and you have to teach the lesson even though you know it's boring. But beyond that, when you are a leader, you should do everything in your power to keep the audience engaged. If people are falling asleep, that is a sign that something is

going wrong; if people aren't paying attention or try to sneak out, all of these are signs that something is going wrong. Whereas if they are nodding their heads and smiling, you know that they are on the same page as you.

10. You must create a sense of trust, and the best way to do this is with honesty. I am extremely open and honest about my life and my experiences with my audience. In my emails and books, I share very personal stories that are all true. Every single story that I share is something that actually happened to me. I get emails from people asking if they are real, and they all are. I am fortunate enough to live a life where so many crazy things have happened that I have enough examples for all of my books. Leading with honesty builds trust. Being open and emotional first, telling something real, will make it easier for people to follow you and be open and honest as well.

Writing Skills

Becoming a better writer will help you become more influential. When speaking, I can influence a large crowd, but I can also speak one-on-one and influence one person. When I host a webinar online, my software can handle one thousand people for each live training session; if I max out the software, I can influence one thousand people at the same time. As a speaker, you are limited by time, and you can only affect the people that are with you at the same time. But as a writer, you can affect far more people. Every time I sell a book, I start a new conversation with a new person, just like the one we are having right now. That is the power of written communication.

Written communication – being convincing and being able to influence and persuade in writing – is often called copywriting. The simplest way to master copywriting is to find classic sales material and ads, and copy them by hand so you can see, observe, and replicate great convincing and motivational writing. This is how I became better at writing: practice, practice, practice. I have over six hundred classic ads that I like to copy from. I have put together a giant PDF that you can get on my website (there is a link on the Influence &

Persuasion page), so you can download that anytime you want and use it to practice becoming a more persuasive writer. It does take some time, but if you put in just thirty minutes a day, within six months you will become one of the best influential writers in the entire world.

To become a better writer, there are two key elements beyond the principles of copywriting. The first is looking at the detail, the small picture: this is where you work on punctuation, grammar, spelling, and sentence structure. These are things that an editor can help you with. Problems in these areas can block your communication. If you have every word misspelled, people will not listen to the rest of what you have to say, so these parts are quite important. Fortunately, there are many software tools and spellchecks out there to help you get through this process. If you received a resume from the best employee in the world, but it was full of spelling and grammar mistakes, would you hire that person? The fact that you even had to think about it is a sign that you need to look at the micro-level communication, the small picture.

Second, at the macro level, there are organization, coherence, clarity, style, and substance. These large elements are more about the actual message. We have the communication, our spelling, and grammar, and then we have the structure of the message itself, the copy, the convincing elements.

Micro-Level Writing Elements

- Punctuation
- Grammar
- Spelling
- Sentence Structure

Macro-Level Writing Elements

- Organization
- Coherence
- Clarity
- Style
- Substance

Let's take a closer look at some of the macro-level elements listed here.

Organization

Organization is the structure and the flow of your argument. When your structure is choppy, or things happen out of order, people won't fall into alignment.

A great way to learn this is by following the structure of classic ads or looking at the structure of similar arguments.

When copywriting, I start by reverse engineering. I look at a similar letter or similar argument, and I study the structure of that argument. If you want to see good organization in live action, watch an infomercial. Although they are speaking out loud, the entire script is written as an argument designed to get you to purchase.

The amount of science that goes into an infomercial is astounding. Every word is analyzed, everything is done in a certain order, and their tests cost hundreds of thousands or even millions of dollars as they dial in and perfect the message.

What you say is often not nearly as important as the order in which you say it. Structure is critical when it comes to influence.

Coherence and Conciseness

Your argument, your story, your letter should all flow and make sense together. When designing a sales letter, which is the ultimate example of written influence, it is very tempting to use loads of evidence.

The first thing I do when preparing an argument is look for as much evidence as I can. I just finished working on a medical project for a new supplement, and my research document is sixty-seven pages of links, quotes, and medical references, all from medical studies or highly reputed doctors or hospitals – all to get the perfect message right. The final sales letter, the final message itself will be only ten or twenty pages long, and it won't be all evidence.

It is important to cut away the extra evidence and the boring science that loses your audience. Finding that perfect balance is critical. As much as it starts with writing, it comes down to the editing. You cut away the fat. Sometimes, when I edit, I have to use an ax to chop away so much extraneous material. Remove anything that doesn't benefit your argument or your story. If you have a sentence that feels extra, cut it out.

Clarity

It is very hard to self-analyze clarity. Fortunately, it is very easy for anyone else to provide feedback. With anything written, you can show it to someone in your life; if they say, "I don't understand this part," or, "What does this mean," you know you there is a problem with clarity. It is usually the first thing people say, "I don't understand this section, what does this mean? What does this word mean?"

You can have the greatest argument in the world, but if you use words that people don't understand or if people get lost, you can lose everything. Sometimes people get lost early on, and they spend the rest of your argument trying to figure out what that first part meant.

Planning Your Writing

How can I become a better writer? How can I become a more structured copy-writer? How can I become more influential when I write things down?

In addition to the long-term exercise of hand-copying amazing arguments from the past, taking the time to write down the structure for anything you are going to say in advance will give you a leg up. Oftentimes, I write down the outline for a book – just the chapter titles, these are the twenty things I want to talk about. Then, when I look back at that structure, I can delete at least three of them because they are extraneous.

How to Plan Your Writing

Doing a bit of outlining before you start writing will help you be more effective. There are a few steps to go through when you are planning your writing.

1. Identify your purpose. Why are you writing this? What is your goal? Whenever I look at a website, book, article, or blog post, I say to the writer, "What is your goal? What do you want someone to do after they read this?" You need to choose a single goal; if you have five different goals, then none of them will be accomplished.

My goal, when you read this entire book, is for you to give me your email address; that allows us to start a communication. That is my only goal with this book – I want to give you great information, and I want to help you become a more influential and persuasive person.

You should have the same goal for everything you work on. If you are writing a review of your product, the goal is for people to click on the link and buy the product so you get a commission. If you are writing a landing page or a squeeze page on your website, the goal is to get that email address. If you are writing an ad for a newspaper, the goal is to get the readers to call a phone number. Knowing your goal will help you to drive your writing in a set direction.

2. Who is your audience? Think about the demographics of your audience. What do they have in common – are they all men, or all women? Are they all young parents? Are they grandparents? Are they young, single professionals? Do they live in the city or the country-

side? Do they love technology or hate it? The more you define your audience, the easier it is to write a message they would listen to.

3. What is your main message? If your reader walks away with one lesson, what is it? What is the most important part of your entire story? We have the purpose, which is what you want for yourself, we know the audience, and now we have the message, which is what you want for the reader.

4. Make sure that you are using the best format. Depending upon your audience, a more casual message will sometimes be more well-received. When you are writing to professionals, you have to write in an extremely formal way. If you are trying to convince a bunch of doctors about a new medical treatment, writing casually will not work. What they expect is very dry and very boring, with a huge quantity of medical references and lots of scientific backup for your argument. Know your audience and communicate in the best way for them.

5. Plan out the structure of your writing. There are a lot of different methods and techniques you can use to create a mind map or outline, such as diagrams and charts. Find a system that works for you and stick with it. I am a heavy mind mapper, and lately I have been doing a lot of outlining by hand, so now I have three different notebooks full of handwritten notes. I have started to shift more to outlining this way for my table of contents and my big picture outlining. Just having some section headings and bullet points, and knowing what you are going to talk about in each section can make it very easy for you to work your way through a speech or a story. You don't have to have everything written out in advance, but a bit of a structure will make it easier for you to do effective writing.

Reflection Questions

Below are some questions to help you reflect on how you have planned your writing up to this point, and what steps you will take in the future. You should write your thoughts on the questions in your Influence and Persuasion Journal.

1. How much effort have you made in the past to plan your

writing? If you did make some effort in this direction, what else do you think you can do to improve the efficacy of your written communication?
2. If you found planning your writing too tedious in the past, has what you learned in this chapter made you more likely to make the effort?
3. Try to think of a piece of written communication you produced in the past that would have been more effective if you had planned it more thoroughly. If you had to re-do this piece today, what planning steps would you take right now?

Planning Your Writing Exercise

Imagine that you have to produce a carefully-crafted and effective piece of written communication to influence and persuade in order to exert your power of leadership. Once you have decided on all of the elements listed below, write out an outline for the structure of the piece.

- Purpose
- Audience
- Main message(s)
- Format

7

FOSTERING LOYALTY

Loyalty is a two-way street; it is as much an obligation for the leader as it is for the follower. Fostering a sense of loyalty in the people we lead is critical. If people do not feel a sense of loyalty towards you, if they are driven by a different motivation, then they will jump ship at the first opportunity. If people only work for you for the money, they will be out of the door as soon as they get a chance to make more money somewhere else. You want to create stronger emotional bonds than that with your teams.

What is Loyalty?

Let us first try to get a solid grasp of what we mean when we say loyalty. At first, it might seem silly to even have this section – everyone knows what loyalty is. Yet if you ask two different people to define what loyalty is, you will still get two very different definitions.

When I was in high school, I read an article in a magazine about friendship and loyalty. This article said that the best way to test another man's friendship and loyalty is to go on a road trip and see if they stay awake or fall asleep. The friend who goes asleep while you are driving is not a loyal person. I thought it was ridiculous until I ran this test and the person next to me fell asleep. I thought, "Oh, that test is wrong, this guy is really loyal." A few months later he betrayed me profoundly, and I discovered upon more research that he had a pattern of this. So it turns out that test is effective.

Another question of loyalty is: if I get attacked, will you jump in and get involved on my behalf? Will you defend me whether it is an emotional or physical attack? I once had a friend whose buddy was attacked by a bunch of guys in the middle of the night, as they were coming out of a burger joint in England. My friend jumped in and started defending the guy, but he ran away, leaving him behind. My friend ended up losing an eye for a disloyal friend.

He still stayed friends with the guy, despite losing his eye while his buddy was being a coward. That same friend essentially destroyed his business a few years later. My friend had a massively popular website and an amazing forum full of really cool people and great conversations – even I was a member. This guy changed all the passwords and deleted everything. He was so disloyal not only he cost a friend his eye, but also stole his business and destroyed it.

It is important to define what we mean when we think about loyalty. There are some common characteristics and things we look for:

- a sense of commitment or demonstration of that commitment
- a sense that there is an alliance or a two-way street between people
- a willingness to invest yourself to help achieve the other person's goals
- an element of respect – you can't be loyal to someone you don't respect

More than anything else, it is your own definition of loyalty that is important. Is your definition of loyalty someone staying late after work to help finish a project even though you are not paying them overtime? Is your definition of loyalty the boss who takes a pay cut to pay for the workers who work overtime?

I would like you to spend some time thinking about your own definition of loyalty and start bringing that into future conversations. When I talk to people, I quickly tell them my definitions of loyalty. In my life and in most people's life, we all have circles of loyalty. I am more loyal to my wife and children than my extended family; then there is my extended family and then comes my staff. Beyond them, there are my readers and followers. I am not more loyal to you than I am to my wife, I know you don't expect that, and I don't expect the same from you.

Loyalty is influenced by the nature of our relationships. Friend-to-friend loyalty is different from boss-to-employer loyalty. A few years ago, I made the mistake of trying to run my business as a friendship, treating everyone as a part of my family. I said, "You will never get fired, and you will be part of my team forever," and they all basically stopped working. I had people who were being paid thousands of dollars while doing ten or twenty dollars' worth of work. I had employees who would work less than an hour a week. Trying to create a family in the wrong environment meant I had to fire everyone and start over. Now I have purely business relationships with my team, and it's much more effective. We are in alliance with our business goals. Trying to mingle business and family goals failed for me.

Definition of Loyalty Exercise

In your Influence and Persuasion Journal, write down your own definition of loyalty from both sides – from a good employee and from a good boss, or whichever type of leader you're working on becoming.

Reflection Questions

Here are some reflection questions that you can use to begin to think more about loyalty. Write down your responses in your Influence and

Persuasion Journal as well.

1. In the past, what led you to believe other people were loyal towards you? Was it the words they said, the actions they took or was it something else? Looking further down the relationship, were your early assessments right? Did the people you thought were loyal later turn on you or vice versa? Oftentimes we say, "I am a good or bad judge of character," and this is what we mean – are you good or bad at assessing people's levels of loyalty?
2. What sorts of behavior or actions make you think that someone is loyal? What behaviors lead you to think that someone is disloyal or can't be trusted? Do you think that your beliefs are fair? Are your rules for judging someone's loyalty or disloyalty fair?
3. What do you think about my definitions of loyalty? Do you think I am right? Do you disagree with me in certain areas? Do you think you can still be loyal while you sleep in your friend's front seat?

It is ok to disagree with me; not everyone has the same definition of loyalty. What you want is to form alliances with people who have the same definition of loyalty, as it is far easier to do that than to try and convince someone of your own definition of loyalty.

Misconceptions about Loyalty

There are some beliefs people have about loyalty that are just either wrong, incorrect or flawed, and they can lead to problems. Sometimes we define loyalty by certain behaviors that are not real signs of loyalty; they are signs of something else.

Some of these include being overly deferential or almost servile. There are certain leaders who like to surround themselves with brown noses and 'yes-men.' They believe that having followers who agree with everything they say is a sign of loyalty – but it is not.

Someone who is loyal will tell you bad news when you need to hear it; these people will not.

A second flawed definition of loyalty is that your follower or worker will put aside all of their own self-interest and motivation to focus instead on your well-being and self-interest. This is not someone who is loyal; this is a slave, someone who is not in control of themselves – not the sign of someone you can trust.

You don't want to look for this form of loyalty: what you want is someone who is in alliance with you, not someone who is mirroring your beliefs to the detriment of themselves. The best way we can describe this flaw is with the idea that you have to have blind obedience, people who will follow you even when you give them bad advice. This is where we start moving down the path from loyalty into cultishness, where you can tell everyone to drink the Kool-Aid or jump off the bridge, or have people taking actions against their self-interest simply because of blind obedience.

Loyalty comes with a measure of intelligence and active decision-making, so that when people follow you and fall into alignment with you, you know that they are aware of your decision-making process and agree with you. This is how you can have checks and balances in your team, to be sure that when you are about to lead your team off a cliff, someone will say something before you all plummet to your deaths.

You might be thinking to yourself that this section is ridiculous, no one would ever overly serve your team, but take a moment to analyze your behavior. Have there been moments in your life when your followers were too obedient and you liked it just a little bit, or you felt a little bit like a king? I have had a few of those moments in my life, and I think that most other people have had them too.

Sometimes you need to check and analyze your behavior and see if you are requiring or encouraging these behaviors. Are you asking workers to come in on Saturday, even though it is hurting the relationships with their families? Do you force your staff to put the company before their families? This creates a team that works harder because they need the money, but secretly they are all hoping you have an early heart attack. This is not the type of team you want to create – it is certainly not the type of team I want.

Assess Your Loyalty Exercise

Examine your own assumptions and make sure you are fair about how you judge loyalty and disloyalty in your team. Write down in your Influence and Persuasion Journal the instances where you have been a little bit off-track.

Causes of Disloyalty

Loyalty is very important, but it is a two-way street. Many leaders look for loyalty from their staff, but return none; they demand extra time, excellence, and extra work, but they never give anything in return to their staff. One-way loyalty is no loyalty at all. In order to receive loyalty, you must give it first.

There are a couple of massive causes of disloyalty, and if you find any of these in your behavior or in your leadership, excise them now before they become a more serious problem.

The first cause of disloyalty is the perception that you do not recognize your team's accomplishments. This comes from not giving enough compliments or stealing credit for your team's work. It can also come from giving credit to the wrong people. If one person does ninety percent of the work and the other person does ten, but you give each person fifty percent of the credit, you are planting the seed for bitterness and disloyalty.

The second cause is the perception that you are not fair. We know life is not fair – good and bad luck come into the picture, there are things outside of our control, and yet something inside us is constantly striving to see fairness. It can be difficult to generate fairness, but you must always strive towards this.

Third is the perception that you don't trust your team members. This can be expressed in different ways – you don't give them keys, you don't allow them to lock up, or you don't give them access to certain files. We all have levels of trust when it comes to our business assets and secrets; this is why you don't give keys to every employee, but you do give keys to the manager. Increasing trust requires an increase in loyalty from both sides.

Fourth, there are team members that do not feel satisfaction. This can happen when their work is too hard, when the projects take too long, or when the work is too easy, or you have them working on projects that are going nowhere. Sometimes, you work on a project that the client pays you for, but you know they are never going to do anything with it. I have ghostwritten books before that I have found out in the middle of the project that the client had no intention of ever releasing. It is hard to feel a sense of satisfaction when you work on something that you know is just going to end up on the trash heap.

Fifth is the perception that you do not care about the team members, that you have a lack of empathy – you don't care about what makes them human, you don't care about their families, their financial situation, the things they are dealing with. There are certain managers who prioritize the work over everything. For instance, they might say, "We have a meeting every Wednesday, if your anniversary is on Wednesday then you still come to our meeting, and you can celebrate your anniversary on Thursday." There are certain groups that want your loyalty to them to be above all else, and when you do that as a leader, your team is going to stop thinking that you care about them – you don't care that their kid is sick or that you forgot the names of their children. All of these things will be perceived as disloyalty.

Finally, it bears mentioning again that if you take credit for all of the team's work, if you say, "I am so glad that I am such a great success," and you ignore the efforts of your team, don't expect loyalty back from them.

The Significance of Loyalty in Influence and Persuasion

We know that loyalty is important when we are working together, but how does it directly correlate to influence and persuasion? The greater sense of loyalty the audience feels towards you, the easier it is to persuade them. When the leader makes a decision the followers don't quite understand the logic of, if they have enough loyalty they will go along with them. Loyalty will cause people to follow your argument even if they don't actually agree with it. This is often called charisma: the ability to get people to fall into alignment or feel loyalty towards you.

More Reflection Questions

Take a few moments to track out the Influence and Persuasion Journal and look at these reflection questions about the interrelationship between loyalty and influence:

1. If someone towards whom you felt a small amount of loyalty tried to influence you, how open to their influence would you be? How do you think your lack of a sense of loyalty would affect the likelihood you are open to their persuasion?
2. Think about a specific person that you feel very little loyalty towards and imagine trying to persuade them against something. How much would your sense of loyalty color your judgment? Before this chapter, have you ever even thought about the connection between loyalty, influence, and persuasion? What were your initial thoughts, and how have they changed now?
3. If you did think of this connection before, what were your initial thoughts? Have any of your opinions or ideas changed after reading this chapter?
4. How will your new understanding of loyalty in relation to

influence and persuasion help you in your future leadership pursuit and efforts?

Loyalty Exercise

In this exercise, you are going to apply what you have learned to your leadership, and then you are going to use your own past experiences. Complete this activity in your Influence and Persuasion Journal before moving onto the next section.

1. What are the most important things you have learned about loyalty in this section? What are the most important ways loyalty interacts with influence and persuasion? Take your time writing multiple answers or paragraphs to come up with as many different key lessons and memories as you can from this section.
2. How can you apply your new knowledge of loyalty to your leadership, persuasion, and influence efforts? What are practical ways and actions that you can take in the near future? What is something you can do tomorrow and what is something you can do next week to use loyalty to make yourself a more effective influencer?
3. Once you have built out a plan, spend the next two weeks implementing it. Actively try to foster and create more loyalty in the environment around you. Each day, write down notes on your efforts to influence and persuade and the results. Track how your leadership is improving over the next two weeks.
4. Once the two-week period is complete, write down a full reflection page about your experiences and what you have learned, and how you know your life is changing. How can you see your ability to persuade growing and how have you improved as a person?

8
YOUR PERSONAL DEVELOPMENT AS A LEADER

Growing as a person is a critical step in becoming a better influencer and a better leader. Developing yourself professionally and personally will help you improve your results and become a better influencer every day, for the rest of your life.

Professional development is about understanding your field and industry better and becoming more of an expert. As you become more knowledgeable, your team will perceive you as a more effective leader – and in reality you will be, because you have a deeper understanding.

You can improve as a person following a few general rules. Make a decision now to be willing to learn new things, even as you get older, and to be willing to learn from younger people. As we get older, we get more set in our ways, and we don't want to listen to the younger generations, but occasionally they do have a few pearls of wisdom.

Be willing to see yourself as a student and have the humility to realize that, even though you are an expert and have been successful for a long time, there are still things you don't know because no one person can know everything.

Actively seek ways to improve your professional development –

look for courses, training, and other ways to become better at your job and more effective as a leader.

Reflection Questions

Write your answers to these questions on professional development in your Influence and Persuasion Journal.

1. Have you ever taken part in any kind of professional development? What form did the professional development take (for example, was it a class, a lecture, or some other format)?
2. If you have taken part in professional development, how effective did you feel it was for you? Did it help you achieve the goals you had in mind? Do you feel that a different form of professional development would have been more helpful to you? Why?
3. What kind of professional development do you plan on doing in the future? How did you decide on this?

Professional Development Possibilities Exercise

Complete this exercise in your Influence and Persuasion Journal.

1. Brainstorm all your possible future professional development opportunities. Ensure that you take a substantial amount of time to do this, and do a bit of research. Write down different aspects and questions you have about each of the opportunity ideas you come up with.
2. Choose one or two of the ideas you came up with in step 1.
3. Do more intensive research on this idea/these ideas.
4. Write a reflective journal entry on what you have learned, and whether you have come up with any helpful, professional development opportunities.

Emotional Intelligence (EI)

We all know about our IQ, our intelligence quotient, but what about your Emotional Intelligence Level? Some people call it an EQ. The way to measure this score (your ability to connect with people) is through your interpersonal and your intrapersonal skills.

Interpersonal Skills

Interpersonal skills are the skills you use when understanding, communicating, and dealing with other people. People who lack these interpersonal skills and people who have social diseases such as Asperger's or Autism struggle the most in forming connections or understanding how to communicate in ways other people will respond to.

When you don't make the right facial expression, it is very easy to cause miscommunication or misinterpretation. Miscommunication is an easy way to shatter your leadership, and we want to avoid it. Building up your interpersonal skills, your ability to talk and connect with people, is a critical step on the path to influence.

Interpersonal Assessment

Before we dig further into this, take a moment to open up your Influence and Persuasion Journal and assess your current interpersonal skills level. How good are you at walking up to strangers? How good are you at building a rapport? How good are you at expressing yourself or understanding where other people are coming from?

It is a mistake to assume you are born good or not good at communication with people; you can get better at these skills. I was terrible at forming friendships until I was seventeen and studied someone else who was a great leader. These are skills you can learn, not talents you were born with.

If you feel like your interpersonal skills are weak – perhaps you feel frustrated or stuck, you want to get better and can't figure out how – the good news is you can improve, and the process begins by working on your sense of self-awareness.

Whenever you feel like you made an interpersonal mistake, write down what happened in your journal. Try to figure out what caused that mistake, what the results of that mistake were, and how you can avoid repeating it in the future.

Improve Your Interpersonal Skills

In order to help you improve your interpersonal skills development, there are a few steps you can take.

1. Cultivate an optimistic attitude. Misery loves company, but unfortunately company does not love misery. Being optimistic, smiling all the time, and always having a positive attitude can help you overcome many social faux pas and conversational mistakes. People will forgive you for a mistake if your attitude is always positive because they know that your miscommunication was never intentional; they will always give you benefit of the doubt. People will be more receptive to your ideas and opinions, and it will be easier for you to form rapport. You will pull them into a higher emotional state, and they will be happier when they are around you.

2. Consistently and clearly demonstrate your appreciation for the people around you. Whether it is your team, a family member, a co-worker, or anyone else in your sphere of influence, the more people feel appreciated, the more effort they will want to put in. Like Pavlov's dogs salivating for that ringing bell, they will seek your approval because you make them feel good.

3. Practice active listening. We have mentioned this before, and it is worth mentioning it again. Carefully, tentatively and interactively listen to everything people around you have to say. Don't focus on what you are going to say next; focus on hearing, understanding, and absorbing what people are saying. Sometimes you have to repeat back some of what they say or use some of their own language to demonstrate that you are actively listening. This will give you better conversational success.

4. Improve your body language. Study micro expressions and watch the way people move. Find body language leaders to mimic. When I wanted to learn better body language to come across as a bit of a roguish bad boy, I watched video after video and looked at photographs of James Dean, the classic prototype of the American bad boy. He has been dead for a very long time, and yet most Americans know who he is. Although, to be fair, most Americans can only name one of his movies – the man only made three movies, and yet his legend lives on.

The easiest way to master body language is to find someone, a celebrity – whether it is a business person, a chef, an actor, or musician – and mimic what they are doing. This will help you express more dominant and more confident body language. As you start acting as this other person, people will begin to perceive you the same way as they perceive this person.

5. Show genuine consideration. Don't just pretend to care about other people, actually care about them.

6. Look people in the eye. It is extremely difficult to look at people in the eye during a conversation – most people look from eye to eye, to mouth, in a triangle, or they look next to the person instead of looking at the person. Look someone in the eye today and count to five. You will find that it is unbelievably difficult, and if you make it all the way to five, you will form a very powerful connection, and you will see exactly what can happen. After you have performed this activity, write down your results in your Influence and Persuasion Journal.

7. Work on your negotiation skills. There are so many people who are terrible at negotiation. You will find people who talk about how effective they are at communication, but the second there is an opportunity to negotiate they crumble. The first step to negotiate is removing emotion. People who get personally involved or emotionally reactive in a negotiation always lose. Enter environments where you can practice negotiation without true stake. You can only successfully negotiate when you are able to walk away and you don't care. Before you try to negotiate a raise from your boss, go to the television

store and try to negotiate a discount or a free DVD player. If you don't care whether you win or lose, this will give you a feeling of control throughout the negotiation.

8. Think before you speak! We learn this as children, then we immediately forget it. Make a conscious decision to wait five seconds before responding to anything anyone says to you. If you simply wait five seconds, your conversational skills will go through the roof. Oftentimes, we say something and we realize it is inappropriate one second after we said it. If we had just waited, that five-second delay we would have made us catch ourselves before saying something out loud.

9. Continue to work on improving your sense of empathy. Work on caring about other people and try to figure out what they feel and what it is like to be them.

10. Finally, be friendly. When you project friendliness, people will walk up to you; they will open up to you, and you will find it easy to form conversational connections.

More Reflection Questions

Write your answers to these questions on interpersonal skills in your Influence and Persuasion Journal.

1. How good would you say that your interpersonal skills currently are? If you think they are lacking, in which areas do you think they especially need improvement?
2. Name three of the areas listed above that you think you are strongest in. Explain your opinion and give examples, if you can.
3. Name three of the areas listed above that you think you need a lot of improvement in. Explain your opinion and give examples, if you can.

Active Listening Practice Exercise

1. Choose something to listen to. It can be a documentary, a TED lecture, or something else of your choice. Make sure that you are able to pause the recording when necessary.
2. Listen to your chosen recording. At short intervals, pause the recording and write active listening notes in your Influence and Persuasion Journal. This means that you need to write down a summary of what you have heard, in your own words. You also need to write a reflection on what you have heard, setting out your thoughts.

Intrapersonal Skills

When thinking of influence and persuasion, we usually think about how we interact with other people. We think about technique, skill, and strategy. How can I put together the right combination of words to make other people do the things that I want? That's probably what you thought of when you went to buy this book, "I'd like more influence and the ability to persuade." Before we can convince other people, we need to convince ourselves.

The process of persuasion starts with understanding ourselves, and the best way to describe this is self-confidence or belief in yourself. When you are convincing other people, when you are in the process of persuading, you are selling a product, and you are the product. The more you believe in the product, the more people will fall in line with you. Therefore, the more you believe in yourself, the easier it is for people to believe in you as well.

This is why criminals, con men, and politicians are so supremely confident. Their confidence is what breeds trust. Working on developing your intrapersonal skills will help you be a more effective persuader. Begin by asking yourself this simple question: do you have belief in yourself?

If this is an area you feel stuck or need to improve, the easiest way to build your self-confidence is to create an imaginary version of yourself – the 2.0 version of yourself – and decide this is how your future self will act. As you play this role, you will act like a more confident person. Your intrapersonal skills will be more effective, and you will also believe that you are this new person. By faking it until you make it, by pretending to be a better version of yourself, you will become that better self. That is the power of working on your intrapersonal skills.

Even More Reflection Questions

Below are some reflection questions on intrapersonal skills. Write your answers to these questions in your Influence and Persuasion Journal.

1. How strong would you say your intrapersonal skills are at this point? Have you ever really thought of the question of intrapersonal skills?
2. How good are you at spending time alone without feeling lonely? Do you enjoy your own company?
3. How often do you have what you feel are deep and meaningful insights? Do you pay attention to your own mind? Would you describe yourself as a mindful person?
4. Do you keep a journal or diary? If you do, do you enjoy doing so? Why or why not? If you do not, have you ever done so? If you have, did you enjoy it? What did you get out of it? Do you think you would ever keep a journal or diary again?

Understanding Your Team Members as Individuals

Work and business tend to take up a lot of our time; we get distracted, overwhelmed. We are so busy trying to implement every step to make our businesses profitable and successful that we fail in the smaller steps. We fail to notice who our teams are and we sometimes forget that we are individuals, humans, that they have hopes and dreams. If your assistant has a sick child, her attention will be shifted, and it will affect her performance.

If you call out a team member for inferior performance when they are going through something in their personal life, they will probably never forgive you. When I was working for company and had to have a medical procedure that nearly cost me my life, it turned out the doctor was pulling an insurance scam and was willing to very nearly kill me to make an extra couple hundred dollars. When I went back to work and spoke to my employers over needing to get a note from this doctor, I explained that he had nearly killed me out of this greed and I didn't want to go back to this doctor. A few months later, they said, "Hey, you forgot to submit your paperwork for that time you were off, to prove that you went to the doctor." Then I said, "Guess what, I hate you," and I became the worst employee they ever had. The second you forget that one of your staff members or the people you are working with has a problem in their lives, you can plant a seed that will last forever.

I don't use the word "hate" very often, but that is a word I used for my employers at that time. I thought, "You know what? Fine. You want to play that game? I'll play that game too." And I took an unbelievable number of sick days and an unbelievable number of paid holidays – I did all sorts of things. I pushed them over the edge until I finally quit, after I had obtained everything I could out of them. I got every paid sick day, every paid vacation day, and every paid "emergency" day – I probably put in forty percent of the work I was paid for that year.

The moment they made the bad decision to disregard my terrible medical experience, basically saying, "We don't care about you as a human," I said, "Fair enough, then I don't care about you as a boss." Most companies are like this; they don't care that your child is sick, they don't care if you live or die, and this is why everyone steals office supplies. This is why people take sick days all the time when they are not sick. When you establish a relationship where you don't care about your workers, they won't care about you.

Larger companies can get away with this, but when you are a smaller company, you really can't afford to lose fifteen percent of your profit due to company theft. Larger companies would rather not fix the problem, and instead they build it into their budget. When you are smaller, it is much more important to care about your staff.

I have a very small team, and I try to keep track of each person that I work with. I try to keep track of their current relationship status, any health problems that they have, and if they have children, I like to keep track of how they are because it matters to people. It really matters to people that you remember their child's birthday or name. I'm not perfect, and I would love to say I'm the best boss in the world, but just like you, I can do better.

The more you have empathy for your team and actually care about them as people, the more they will go the extra mile for you, the more they will do every task that you ask and then think about billing you rather than writing down exactly how much it's going to cost. There are some people that work for you and when you go, "Hey, can you take care of this?" They say it's going to be overtime; they are always thinking that way, and that's because you haven't established a strong relationship with love.

Be a Better Leader

You want to establish the habit of seeing your team members as individuals and letting them know you see them that way. There are a couple of ways you can communicate your appreciation or recognition for them.

1. You can learn each of their talents and find them projects or encourage them to build their talents in different ways. If you have a team member who is an artist, you can encourage them to work on a logo or design something for the website.

2. Recognize their achievements when you have a team member who graduates from a program or accomplishes something. You want to make sure everyone knows about them and let them feel good about it.

3. Communicate how integral each member is to the team. Let each team member know that the other team members are important. When you tell Sally how great Jessica is, it makes them both feel good. It feels good if you tell me how great I am to my face, but if I know you are saying good things about me to other people, that makes me feel even better. We don't want anyone to feel left out.

As your team gets larger and expands past five or ten people, it becomes very difficult to handle each of these tasks individually. This is why once companies reach a certain size, you then hire a manager to be charge of the other staff. Keeping track of birthdays, holidays, sick days, and needs gets complicated, and that is why you eventually build a Human Resources department.

HR departments were originally all about taking care of people's needs – making sure that everyone got paid on time, that everyone's sick days were taken care of, that health insurance stuff was all handled correctly and so on. Nowadays, it seems like HR departments are only there to make it hard to hire and fire people, and no longer give everyone a good experience. This is unfortunate, because the original intention of the department, back when it was called payroll, was to make sure everyone got what they wanted and what they deserved – it was about benefitting everyone, but unfortunately those days have faded into the sands of time.

WHAT WE'VE LEARNED

We certainly have covered and learned a lot about the concepts of influence, persuasion, leadership, charisma, and team management in this book. I am really excited to see what the future holds for you, to see you implement the lessons in this book and to start to feel like you are the one holding the rudder of your destiny.

In chapter one, we talked about the fundamentals of leadership and the characteristics and features that define great and effective leaders. We talked about how influence and leadership are connected to each other; one without the other is impossible.

In chapter two, we went on and learned about the importance of shared values and vision in effective leadership. When the leader and the team are headed towards the same goal, it is easier for them to stay in alignment, and it is easier for them to hit those success points. We talked about the importance of team connection and team dynamics – how that builds the strength of your company and leads to more success. Then you wrote about a leader that you admire, and we made a plan to create a shared vision and values for your own team.

In chapter three, we talked about the art of persuasion, some of the tactics you can use to become more persuasive, and factors that will help increase your credibility. Don't forget that you completed the "persuasion in everyday life" exercise. This exercise helped you to better understand how you can put your knowledge of influence and persuasion into everyday practice, how you can implement the lessons of this book. Reading a book about persuasion is great, but becoming more persuasive is far better.

In chapter four, we began to talk about positive workplace culture. This is where you are leading a team in a business environment. We discussed ways that you can lead your team effectively and make sure that they are working together effectively, being aware of problems before they begin to grow into something bigger. This is so you can nip those little problems in the butt so your team can become more effective, like a well-oiled machine.

In chapter five, we looked at team dynamics. What are the characteristics of a bad team, what are signs that there are problems and signs that the team isn't going to last, and how problems in the team always come back to being the leader's or the boss's problem. Bad leadership leads to bad team dynamics, but a bad leader often doesn't realize they caused the problem themselves, and they end up firing the best employee instead of the worst employee. We explored some of the root causes of these dynamics so that you can check your team and notice problems early on, so they don't grow and poison your company.

In chapter six, we talked about communication, although we already know that communication is important in persuasion. We dug a little deeper, we talked about active listening, and we did some active listening exercises. We also talked about strong speaking skills and possibly overcoming your fear of public speaking, which is one of the most common fears in the West. Beyond persuasive speaking, we also talked about persuasive writing. The ability to write a sales letter or message that convinces people to take action. This is a very important skill, and it is just as important to be able to persuade via the written word as it is via the spoken word.

In chapter seven, we discussed loyalty as a two-way street. How many leaders look for subservience and servility but forget that you have to give your team as much loyalty as you ask back from them? When you have an uneven or misplaced relationship, everything will crumble, and your team will turn against you. We began to explore how loyalty is a critical component of influence and persuasion, and we completed an awesome exercise where you began to brainstorm some ideas about loyalty. You learned how to start taking immediate action to being to increase the loyalty you give your team so that they immediately give you more loyalty back.

Finally, in chapter eight, we talked about your personal journey to becoming a better leader – someone who has the power of influence and who people follow because they want to. It is important to focus on both your personal and professional development; when you grow as a person, you become a better leader. You began to reflect on some of the unexplored areas of professional development, how you can become better at your job, more knowledgeable, more of an expert, and how that expertise will bring more people into alignment with you.

Then, of course, we discussed the significance of emotional intelligence. In the areas of interpersonal skills, we covered how you relate to other people, and on intrapersonal skills, how you relate to yourself. We mentioned self-confidence: the more you believe in yourself, the more other people will believe in you. A leader without self-confidence will always fail.

THE END IS JUST ANOTHER BEGINNING

We have covered a lot of ground in this book, and I am very proud of you. Most people who buy books never finish them. Even though this book is short (it is one of the shortest books that I have written, so that it is more manageable), most people won't finish it or participate in the exercises. By finishing the book and taking the action steps, you have already moved into the top one percent. You have the knowledge, the tools, and the skillset to become more influential and more persuasive. Now the ball is in your court, and it is time to take action.

I am excited that we went on this journey together, and I am excited to see how things go for you. As with all of my books, please leave your feedback on Amazon. Please email me with questions or moments where you get stuck, or if you need help with an exercise. This is cooperative effort, not a one-way street. If you email me with a situation where you are stuck or facing a challenge, I will help you break through that.

You are now a member of the Serve No Master Tribe. Reading one of my books brings you into my family, and I have an obligation to help you succeed. I don't want to just give you the information and leave you on your own; that's how books worked two hundred years ago, those days are past. You can send me an email, and I will send you a reply within a day. I check my email every single morning. We are on this journey together, and I see great things for you; when you have those great successes, I want you to email me and let me know all about them.

Thank you so much for letting me be a part of your journey, and I can't wait to see what the future holds for you.

DID YOU TAKE THE ASSESSMENT?

Thank you so much for reading *Influence and Persuasion* Before you forget, please take this quick assessment. This will help us to work together and maximize your results. Please go now to:

https://servenomaster.com/persuasive

MORE INFORMATION

Throughout this book I mentioned other books, images, links, and additional content. All of that can be found at:

https://servenomaster.com/influencer

You don't have to worry about trying to remember any other links or the names of anything mentioned in this book. Just enjoy the journey and focus on taking control of your destiny.

FOUND A TYPO?

While every effort goes into ensuring that this book is flawless, it is inevitable that a mistake or two will slip through the cracks.

If you find an error of any kind in this book, please let me know by visiting:

ServeNoMaster.com/typos

I appreciate you taking the time to notify me. This ensures that future readers never have to experience that awful typo. You are making the world a better place.

ABOUT THE AUTHOR

Born in Los Angeles, raised in Nashville, educated in London - Jonathan Green has spent years wandering the globe as his own boss - but it didn't come without a price. Like most people, he struggled through years of working in a vast, unfeeling bureaucracy. And even though he was 'totally crushed' when he got fired, it gave him the chance to reappraise his life and rebuild it from scratch.

Since 2010, he's been making a full-time living on the Internet - helping brick and mortar business owners promote themselves on the Internet, helping men and women find true love, ghostwriting best sellers for some of the biggest publishers in the world and much, much more.

Thanks to smart planning and personal discipline, he was more successful than he could have possibly expected. He traveled the world, helped friends and family, and moved to an island in the South Pacific.

Now he's passing his knowledge onto the rest of the world as host of a weekly podcast that teaches financial independence, networking with the world's most influential people, writing epic stuff online, and traveling the world for cheap.

His hobbies include kayaking, surfing, and building empires. He currently has a loving girlfriend, and two wonderful kids who love the ocean (almost!) as much as he does.

Find out more about Jonathan at:
ServeNoMaster.com

BOOKS BY JONATHAN GREEN

Serve No Master Series

Serve No Master

Breaking Orbit

20K a Day

Control Your Fate

Habit of Success Series

PROCRASTINATION

Influence and Persuasion

Love Yourself

Color Depression Away

ADULT COLORING BOOKS BY JONATHAN GREEN AND ARTOFCOLORINGBOOK.COM

Complex Adult Coloring Books

The Dinosaur Adult Coloring Book

The Dog Adult Coloring Book

The Celtic Adult Coloring Book

The Space Adult Coloring Book

Irreverent Coloring Books

Dragons Are Bastards

ONE LAST THING

Reviews are the lifeblood of any book on Amazon and especially for the independent author. If you would click five stars on your Kindle device or visit this special link at your convenience, that will ensure that I can continue to produce more books. A quick rating or review helps me to support my family and I deeply appreciate it.

Without stars and reviews, you would never have found this book. Please take just thirty seconds of your time to support an independent author by leaving a rating.

Thank you so much!

To leave a review go to ->

https://servenomaster.com/influencereview

Sincerely,
Jonathan Green
ServeNoMaster.com

www.ingramcontent.com/pod-product-compliance
Lightning Source LLC
Chambersburg PA
CBHW060046230426
43661CB00004B/670